Advance Praise for *Simply Imperfect*

Simply Imperfect is an inspiring breath of fresh air and freedom in our consumerist society — a book that awakens us to the beauty of life's imperfections. In looking beyond the contemporary world of shallow materialism, Lawrence invites us to celebrate the depth and elegant grace of authentic simplicity, both in our possessions and in our awareness of life.

— Duane Elgin, author of *Voluntary Simplicity*
and *The Living Universe*

Do those TV home shows where every kitchen and bath "needs updating" drive you bats? Are you very DISinclined to follow the latest fashion trends? Do you find grace and beauty in things that are handmade and well-worn rather than in things that are new and flashy? Then I predict you will be simply delighted to read *Simply Imperfect* and discover the Japanese aesthetic known as wabi-sabi.

— Cheryl Long, editor-in-chief, *Mother Earth News*

Robyn Griggs Lawrence applies an ancient Japanese philosophy to today's world and comes up with relevant, poetic solutions for modern living. This book is a must-read for anyone looking to simplify and create peace — and respite — in their homes.

— Wanda Urbanska, author, *The Heart of Simple Living:
7 Paths to a Better Life* and coauthor, *Less is More*

Simply Imperfect is a meditation, a path to be walked upon slowly, a breath to be inhaled and exhaled consciously. Its use of the ancient Japanese philosophy "wabi-sabi", as a design point of view and, more importantly, a way of being in the world, returns us to the simplicity and beauty of home-made, home-grown, naturally inspired, and all that the cyber-world of virtual and superficial realities has seemingly forgotten. Wabi-sabi is the breeze through a screen door, the patina of a copper roof, the smoothing and grooving of an old wooden table. It is life unfolding without the need to change or correct it… it's simply, and wonderfully, imperfect.

— Skaie Knox, editor-in-chief blogger, DiggersList.com

Simply Imperfect is the ideal antidote to the strident, guilt-ridden environmentalism of yesteryear. Robyn Griggs Lawrence gives readers the perspective they need to really enjoy their homes and their lives while making changes in their routines that benefit the planet, and their peace of mind. This is a wise book that I find myself revisiting again and again.

— Bryan Welch, publisher, *Mother Earth News,*
Utne Reader, Natural Home & Garden,
and author, *Beautiful and Abundant:*
Building the World We Want (2010)

simply imperfect

revisiting the
wabi-sabi house

ROBYN GRIGGS LAWRENCE

NEW SOCIETY PUBLISHERS

Cover design by Diane McIntosh
Cover Photo © Povy Kendal Atchison
Interior book design/layout by Gregory Green and John McKercher
Interior photography by Joe Coca, unless otherwise noted

Printed in Canada. First printing April 2011.

Paperback ISBN: 978-0-86571-691-1   eISBN: 978-1-55092-470-1

Inquiries regarding requests to reprint all or part of *Simply Imperfect*
should be addressed to New Society Publishers at the address below.

To order directly from the publishers, please call toll-free (North America)
1-800-567-6772, or order online at www.newsociety.com

Any other inquiries can be directed by mail to:

New Society Publishers
P.O. Box 189, Gabriola Island, BC V0R 1X0, Canada
(250) 247-9737

New Society Publishers' mission is to publish books that contribute in fundamental ways to building an ecologically sustainable and just society, and to do so with the least possible impact on the environment, in a manner that models this vision. We are committed to doing this not just through education, but through action. Our printed, bound books are printed on Forest Stewardship Council-certified acid-free paper that is **100% post-consumer recycled** (100% old growth forest-free), processed chlorine free, and printed with vegetable-based, low-VOC inks, with covers produced using FSC-certified stock. New Society also works to reduce its carbon footprint, and purchases carbon offsets based on an annual audit to ensure a carbon neutral footprint. For further information, or to browse our full list of books and purchase securely, visit our website at: www.newsociety.com

Library and Archives Canada Cataloguing in Publication

Lawrence, Robyn Griggs
Simply imperfect : revisiting the Wabi-Sabi house / Robyn Griggs Lawrence.
Includes index.
Original ed. published. as: The Wabi-Sabi house. New York : Clarkson Potter, 2004.
ISBN 978-0-86571-691-9
1. Interior decoration — Psychological aspects. 2. Interior decoration — Themes, motives.
3. Zen Buddhism — Influence. 4. Design — Japan. 5. Wabi. 6. Sabi. I. Lawrence, Robyn Griggs.
Wabi-Sabi house. II. Title.
NK2113.L39 2011   747.01'9
C2011-901464-5

NEW SOCIETY PUBLISHERS
www.newsociety.com

MIX
Paper from
responsible sources
FSC® C011825

To Suzanne Griggs, with love

My mom's not wabi-sabi at first glance.
She's much more refined than rustic.
But she taught me gracious manners—
the most important of all wabi traits.
Thank you, Mom.

～

I also dedicate this book, with love and respect,
to the honorable Japanese people. A portion of the
proceeds from sales of this book will be donated to the
Tzu Chi Foundation, a Buddhist nonprofit humanitarian
organization providing relief to the devastated region.

～

Every spirit builds itself a house;
and beyond its house, a world;
and beyond its world, a heaven.

Ralph Waldo Emerson

Rustic yet refined, wabi-sabi celebrates imperfection.

contents

wabi-sabi *is...*   wabi-sabi *isn't...*

wabi-sabi *is...*	wabi-sabi *isn't...*
Dry leaves	Cherry blossoms
Bare branches	Floral arrangements
Wild flowers	Roses
Handmade items	Machine-made items
Weathered wood	Plastic laminate
Crumbling stone	Polished marble
Rice paper	Plate glass
Clay	Porcelain
Vintage finds	Designer products
Cobblestones	Concrete
Adobe	Steel
Arts and Crafts	Rococo
Flea markets	Discount stores
Salvaged finds	Custom creations
Hemp	Polyester
Burlap	Velvet
Recycled glass	Crystal
Native landscaping	Kentucky bluegrass
Natural linoleum	Vinyl
Natural plaster	Drywall
Natural light	Fluorescents
Clotheslines	Electric dryers
Hand mixers	Food processors

Carl Wycoff

Kate NaDeau's hand-built cottage furnished with flea market finds epitomizes wabi-sabi living.

Carolyn Bates

part 1 | discover

The voyage of
discovery is not
in seeking new
landscapes but in
having new eyes.

— Marcel Proust

CHAPTER 1

chasing wabi-sabi

I LANDED AT KATE NADEAU'S SWEET, RUSTIC STONE HOUSE ON A hillside near Belfast, Maine, while scouting houses and gardens to feature in *Natural Home* magazine. I had gone to see Kate's gardens, bountiful with vegetables, flowers and herbs that she sells at the farmers' market under the moniker Stone Soup Farm, but I couldn't stop asking about the stone cottage. Kate and her former husband, both disciples of back-to-the-landers Scott and Helen Nearing, had built the house over the course of five years, she told me. They had placed every stone with their own hands. Kate was clearly proud of her house, but I had to invite myself to see inside. Kate said she didn't think a magazine editor would appreciate the way she lived. I told her that *Natural Home* wasn't just another home décor magazine. Eventually, she let me in.

Kate's home was charming, appointed with cozy, flea-market furniture and dumpster finds. Her 1930s stove had narrow rust rivulets in its chipped and yellowing enamel, but it worked well enough to accomplish regular meals as well as some heavy canning and preserving. The wooden dining chairs didn't match, and a wine-colored armchair near the woodstove had seen better days. Herbs and flowers hung drying from beams overhead. I wanted to sit down and spend the rest of the afternoon in the sunlight at the kitchen table, helping Kate snap beans. I loved her casual, frugal decorating style; nothing was new, and everything had a story and a reason for being in her home. I asked about a rusty grate hanging on the wall.

"Oh, that," she said. "That is *so* wabi-sabi."

"Wobby *what?*" I asked.

She described *wabi-sabi* as the Japanese art of appreciating things that are imperfect, primitive and incomplete, and she sent me home with a slim volume, *Wabi-Sabi for Artists, Designers, Poets & Philosophers*, by Leonard Koren — one of the most important gifts I've ever received. Before I even read Koren's book, I knew I'd been wabi-sabi all my life. This ancient Japanese concept of revering gracefully weathered, rusty things exactly matched my own proclivities. Finally, I would have a word I could use when my mother asked whether I was going to paint those old wooden French doors or replace the 1940s enamel table I worked on with a real desk. I delved more deeply and found that décor was wabi-sabi's surface, one facet of a philosophy that promotes attention, reverence, generosity and respect — the foundation of a happy home.

Wabi-sabi isn't a "look," like French country or shabby chic. Intimately tied to Zen Buddhism and the Japanese Way of Tea, it's a subtly spiritual philosophy that offers a path toward home as sanctuary, a simple place devoid of clutter, disturbance and distraction — including the voices in our heads that attach all sorts of tasks and to-do lists to home. Wabi-sabi doesn't suggest we ignore these tasks, but it does say we can pay attention when attention is due and stop worrying about them when we should be enjoying dinner with our families. It focuses on things as they are, right now. Everything in our homes — from the breakfast table to the attic windows — presents an opportunity to see beauty. Wabi-sabi is a lens.

The essence of education is not to transfer knowledge; it is to guide the learning process, to put responsibility for study into the students' own hands.

— Tsunesaburo Makiguchi

I went to Japan to learn more about wabi-sabi. I found it in the crowded, twisted alleyways of Tokyo's Asakusa district, where I was always lost and strangers would walk me to my destination if they didn't speak English. I understood it every time I watched a store clerk carefully wrap a jar of pickles in pretty paper, turning it into a small moment of celebration. I felt it when my host or hostess would turn my shoes around to face the door, so they would be easier to slip into when I left.

I feasted on wabi-sabi. In Japan, simple food — fish, rice, vegetables, seaweed and vinegar — becomes a visual feast, honoring the guests, the food, the dishes and even the utensils. There's nothing more beautiful than pan-seared hake's golden-brown edges picking up the rusty flecks of the platter it's on or five thin slices of raw tuna and a dab of bright green wasabi fanned on an opalescent shell-shaped plate. On a hot summer day, a smooth, thin square of chilled tofu (*hiyayakko*), floating on half-melted ice chunks in a shallow bamboo bowl, is sublime.

Greek writer Lafcadio Hearn, who explored late-19th-century Japan extensively, described the Japanese culture as having "an ethical charm reflected in the common life of the people." According to Hearn, "the commonest incidents of everyday life are transfigured by a courtesy at once so artless and so faultless that it appears to spring directly from the heart, without any teaching." That generous attention to the moment, so prevalent throughout Japan, is my understanding of wabi-sabi.

I traveled to Shigaraki, an ancient pottery center, to visit Buddhist priest and tea master Shiho Kanzaki. Kanzaki-san's exquisite vases, pots and tea bowls, fired in traditional wood-fired Anagama kilns, embody wabi-sabi's very essence. Over lunch with Kanzaki-san and his wife in a weathered Shigaraki tea house, we stopped before each course to admire the pottery. The bowls and plates had been made by Kanzaki-san's apprentices, and he quietly pointed out the color variations and the markings left by ash when the dishes were fired. We admired how the rustic acorn-colored bowls embraced lightly

In Japanese, the same character used to write *tsukaeau*, "to be of service to one another," can also be read as *shiawase*, or "happiness."

Robert Compton's wood-fired pottery belies his wabi-sabi mastery.

wabi

Enduring poverty in life
I prepare fire on the hearth
and enjoy the profound touch of Tea.
      — Matuo Basho

Wabi stems from the root *wa*, which means harmony, peace, tranquility and balance. In early Japanese poetry, *wabi* meant sad, desolate and lonely, but also simple, humble by choice and in tune with nature.

Until Zen Buddhism became widespread in the 14th century, wabi was a pejorative term used to describe cheerless, miserable outcasts. As respect for monks' and hermits' spiritual asceticism grew, wabi became respectful — even revered. Sixteenth-century tea master Jo-o described a wabi tea man as someone who feels no dissatisfaction even though he owns no Chinese utensils. Wabi is "the joy of the little monk in his wind-torn robe," a man content with very little, free from greed, indolence and anger.

Desolate undertones still cling to the word *wabi*, sometimes used to describe "the helpless feeling you have when waiting for your lover." It's a diffuse, elusive concept that's less verbal than emotive, so subtle that you almost miss it. "No other word could be more ambiguous in meaning than wabi," Kazue Kyoichi wrote in *Wabicha no Keifu* in 1973. "It's impossible to explain in other words."

Sabi, meaning "the bloom of time," honors rust and the seasonal cycles of birth, decay and rebirth.

sabi

Sabi means "the bloom of time." It connotes natural progression — tarnish, hoariness, rust — the extinguished gloss of what once sparkled. Sabi things carry their years' burdens with dignity and grace: a silver bowl mottles as it oxidizes, a wooden barn gently collapses in on itself, a naked winter bough has stark, muscular beauty. An old car left in a field to rust, as it transforms from an eyesore into a part of the landscape, is the sabi of the United States.

Sabi is based on the Buddhist law of *annica*, or impermanence. Celebrating crumbling, rusty, fraying things acknowledges poetically that nothing (including ourselves and this moment) remains unchanged. Sabi's meaning has changed over time, from its ancient definition "to be desolate" to the more neutral "to grow old." By the 13th century, sabi meant taking pleasure in things that were old and faded. A proverb emerged: "Time is kind to things, but unkind to man."

battered shrimp and soba noodles as steam rose from the thick dark cups holding our strong green tea. Then he turned the conversation to relationship. "Manner and behavior is most important," Kanzaki-san told me. "You always have to think of other persons. If you are always thinking of other persons, you can understand the real wabi-sabi."

The words *wabi* and *sabi* weren't always linked, although they've been together for such a long time that many people use them interchangeably. I met a tea teacher who hates the phrase because the marriage dilutes the two words' separate identities. A Kyoto tea master laughed and said they're thrown together because it sounds catchy, like "ping-pong" and "ding dong." I never did find out exactly why they came together, but as a phrase, *wabi-sabi* becomes more than the sum of its parts.

Honoring modest living and the ever-changing moment, wabi-sabi is the Japanese art of finding beauty in imperfection and profundity in nature, of accepting the natural cycle of growth, decay and death. It's simple, slow and uncluttered — and it reveres authenticity above all. Wabi-sabi is flea markets, not warehouse stores; aged wood, not Pergo; rice paper, not glass. Minimalist wabi-sabi reveres age and celebrates humans over invulnerable machines. It celebrates cracks and crevices and all the marks that time, weather and use leave behind. It reminds us that we are all transient beings — that our bodies and the material world around us are in the process of returning to the dust from which we came. Through wabi-sabi, we learn to embrace both the glory and the impersonal sadness of liver spots, rust and frayed edges, and the march of time they represent.

Wabi-sabi is underplayed and understated, the kind of quiet, undeclared beauty that waits patiently to be discovered. It's a fragmentary glimpse: the branch representing the entire tree, shoji screens filtering the sun, the moon mostly obscured behind a ribbon of cloud. It's a richly mellow beauty that's striking but not obvious, that you

A luxurious house and the taste of delicacies are only pleasures of the mundane world. It is enough if the house does not leak and the food keeps hunger away. This is the teaching of the Buddha — the true meaning of Tea.

— Tea Master Sen no Rikyu

can imagine having around you for a long, long time — Katherine Hepburn versus Marilyn Monroe. For the Japanese, it's the difference between *kirei* — "merely pretty" — and *omoshiroi*, the interestingness that kicks something into the realm of beautiful. (*Omoshiroi* literally means "white-faced," and its meanings range from fascinating to fantastic.) It's the peace found in a moss garden, the musty smell of geraniums, the astringent taste of powdered green tea. My favorite Japanese phrase for describing wabi-sabi is *natsukashii furusato*, "an old memory of my home town." (As more Japanese people have moved from the countryside to Tokyo and Osaka, this phrase has become more prevalent. Even those who never had roots in a small village want the experience; well-off Japanese people can rent prototypical country houses — complete with grandparents — for weekends.)

Sitting quietly,
doing nothing
Spring comes,
and the grass
grows by itself.

— Zenrin, *The Gospel*
According to Zen

many shades of pretty

The Japanese call hidden beauty "ah-ness." Their lexicon is full of rich descriptions for how things (and people) outwardly appear.

Iki: suggestive, coquettish, sexy; mature but young at heart (Betty White)

Hade: bold, exuberant, youthful, gaudy (Lady Gaga)

Jimi: sedate; proper and unobtrusive but rich and expensive (Queen Elizabeth)

Shibui: severe good taste; quiet but distinctive (Norah Jones)

Miyabi: refined sensibility associated with educated tastes (Barack Obama)

Kirakirashii: shining, brilliant, bright, flashing (Jay-Z)

wabibito: be free

Daisetz T. Suzuki, one of Japan's foremost English-speaking authorities on Zen Buddhism and an early interpreter of Japanese culture for Westerners, described wabi-sabi as an active aesthetical appreciation of poverty. He refers to poverty not as we Westerners interpret — and fear — it, but establishes the difference between a Thoreau-like *wabibito* ("wabi person") and a Dickensian *makoto no hinjin*, whose poverty makes him desperate and pitiful.

Wabi-sabi is a celebration of the freedom that comes from shedding the huge weight of attachments and material concerns. "Wabi is to be satisfied with a little hut, a room of two or three tatami mats, like the log cabin of Thoreau," Suzuki wrote, "and with a dish of vegetables picked in the neighboring fields, and perhaps to be listening to the pattering of a gentle spring rainfall."

Spending a quiet afternoon soaking up the sunlight can tune you into wabi-sabi.

In wabi-sabi conversations, the word *authentic* pops up. Everyone, from an authenticity snob who likes certificates to an Eastern-religion seeker who holds authenticity in a completely different realm, has a different idea about what it means. For the purpose of this conversation, I'm defining an authentic wabi-sabi home as one that feels right, without pretense or compromise.

Homemakers in the Depression era knew wabi-sabi (even if they never uttered the phrase). In their homes, things were patched and mended but scrubbed and clean, handmade or chosen and paid for with care. Their linens may have been thin from many washings, but they were crisply white from lemon-juice treatments. Floors may have shown the wear of many feet, but they were swept clean and warmed up with a rug that had faded gracefully from brilliant red to pale rose. Wood had scratches, but it was polished to show off its grain. For those indoctrinated to believe that anything less than perfect should be replaced, our ancestors' hands-on frugality is enlightening — welcome respite in our prosperous age of planned obsolescence.

In a wabi-sabi home, possessions are pared down, and pared down again, to those that are necessary for their utility or beauty (ideally, both). What makes the cut? Useful things: the hand-crank eggbeaters from the flea market that work as well and with much less hassle than electric ones. Things that resonate with the spirit of their makers' hands and hearts: a handmade chair, a six-year-old's lumpy pottery, a lumpy sheep's wool afghan. Pieces of history: sepia-toned ancestral photos, baby shoes, a set of dog-eared Nancy Drew mysteries.

Wabi-sabi interiors are muted, dimly lit and shadowy — giving the rooms an enveloping, womblike feeling — with natural materials that are vulnerable to weathering, warping, shrinking, cracking and peeling. The wabi-sabi palette, limited to browns, blacks, grays, earthy greens and rusts, implies a lack of freedom but actually offers the ultimate creative opportunity. In Japan, kimonos come in 100 shades of gray.

The lapse of time will not turn a bad building into a good, any more than it will turn bad wine into good, but it will most often make a good building very much more beautiful; because it will assimilate it to the surrounding nature, until it seems at last scarcely to have been made, but rather to have grown up from the very soil, an unartificial, inevitable growth.

— William Morris

living right now:
a zen story

Kichibei, a common villager, had a wife whose illness kept her bedridden. Every day, in addition to caring for his wife, he had to cook, sweep and clean his home. One day a neighbor remarked that he must be exhausted. "I do not know what fatigue is," Kichibei replied, "because caring for my wife every day is always both a first experience and a last experience. There is no doing it again, and so I never tire of it."

Depression-era homemakers stitched wabi-sabi into worn but well-loved linens.

I draw water
I carry wood
This is my magic.

— Zen poem

*Wabi-sabi stems from Japanese Tea Ceremony,
an ancient art that endures to this day.*

CHAPTER 2

teasing out its roots: zen, tea and wabi-sabi

WABI-SABI'S ROOTS LIE IN ZEN BUDDHISM, BROUGHT FROM China to Japan by 12th-century traveling monk Esai, who also picked up a few tea seeds while he was there. Zen, with its principles of "vast emptiness and nothing holy," stresses austerity, communion with nature, and reverence for everyday life and everyday mind as the path to enlightenment. Zen monks lived ascetic, often isolated, lives and sat for long periods of concentrated meditation. To help his fellow monks stay awake during these sessions, Eisai taught them how to process tea leaves into a hot drink. Tea had arrived in Japan.

Once it left the monk's hands, tea took on a life of its own. Around the 14th century, the ruling classes developed elaborate rituals that took place in large tea rooms built in a gaudy style known as *shoin*, with imported hanging scrolls and formally arranged tables for vases and incense burners. Tea practitioners proved their wealth and status through their collections of elegant tea utensils and lacquered serving ware during three-day weekends where up to 100 cups of tea — as well as food and sake — were served. All of the day's revered tea masters

Zen's seven ruling principles lead to simple, unpretentious beauty.

pushed the opulent style, to the delight of the Chinese merchants and importers.

In the 15th century, influential tea master and Zen monk Murata Shuko began placing humble, understated utensils made by local artisans next to his finest Chinese porcelain. Saying "It is good to tie a praised horse to a straw-thatched house," he showed the consuming classes that marrying rough with brilliant made both more interesting, and the market for simple bamboo tea servers and hand-shaped tea bowls blossomed. Shuko's successor as Japan's elite tea master, Jo-o, took his master's criticism for rarefied displays a step further by using everyday items such as the *mentsu*, a wooden pilgrim's eating bowl, as a waste-water container, and a Shigaraki *onioke*, a stoneware bucket used in silk dyeing, as a water jar. Jo-o also brought inexpensive unadorned celadon and peasant wares from nearby Korea into the tea room, making the once-upper crust ceremony accessible to the middle classes.

Jo-o's disciple, Sen no Rikyu, is widely credited with creating the quiet, simple ceremony that made it possible for everyone — not just the wealthy — to practice tea. In the 16th century, at the end of several centuries of war and an age of extravagant consumerism, Rikyu's tea ceremony provided a simple, unpretentious oasis that

guiding lights

Zen's seven ruling principles are wabi-sabi's foundation.

Asymmetry (*Fukinsei*): Stiff, frozen symmetry and artificial perfection are imagination's nemesis. More human than godlike, asymmetry is loose and spontaneous.

Simplicity (*Kanso*): Zen is sparse, fresh and neat.

Austerity (*Koko*): Zen asks us to reduce to "the pith of essence," down to the essentials.

Naturalness (*Shizen*): Zen is without pretense or self-consciousness.

Subtle Profundity (*Yugen*): Within Zen lies a deep reserve, a mysterious, shadowy darkness. The hint of soft moonlight through a skylight would be *yugen*.

Freedom from Worldly Attachments (*Datsuzoku*): The Buddha taught non-attachment to life, things and rules. "It is not a strong bond, say the wise, that is made of iron, wood or hemp. Far greater an attachment than that is the longing for jewels and ornaments, children and wives," he said.

Silence (*Seijaku*): Inwardly oriented, Zen embraces the quiet calm of dawn, dusk, late autumn and early spring.

society craved. He served tea in bowls made by anonymous Korean potters and indigenous Japanese craftsmen, and he commissioned pottery from the Raku family, in a style that endures to this day. Rikyu made some of his own utensils out of unlacquered bamboo (as common as crabgrass in Japan, but nowadays a Rikyu original is worth as much as a Leonardo da Vinci painting), and he arranged flowers simply and naturally in bamboo vases and common fishermen's baskets. His tiny tea huts (one-and-a-half-tatami-mats, as opposed to the four-and-a-half- to eighteen-mat norm), based on the traditional farmer's hut of rough mud walls, a thatched roof and organically shaped exposed wood, included a low entryway that forced guests to bow and experience humility as they entered. Rikyu held tea gatherings by dim sunlight, filtered through bamboo lattice screens, or moonlight.

For wealthy merchants and shoguns, this simple, unembellished atmosphere felt like the ultimate luxury — the epitome of high art. For peasants and commoners, it made the art of tea accessible. Through Rikyu's simple ceremony — known as *wabichado* (*chado* means "the way of tea") — everyone, from warlord to peasant, could experience tea. *Wabisuki* ("a taste for all things wabi") took hold of Japan and seeded a revolt against the ruling classes' gaud. Rikyu's "aesthetic of the people" made tea available to even the everyday samurai, who had little in the way of material comforts. Preparing and serving the bitter green leaf became a means for ordinary people to escape for a moment and share a ritual. Tea ceremony became a venue for Japan's finest poets and artists and an important piece of most Zen Buddhists' practice. *Wabichado* endures in Japan to this day.

Though most Westerners don't see the delight in spending four hours kneeling (painfully) to watch someone build a charcoal fire and whisk a bitter green powder known as *matcha* into a froth, *Chanoyu*, or tea (literally "hot water for tea"), has been a revered art in Japan for centuries. We could learn a lot from the ceremony's thoughtfully

The art of chanoyu consists in nothing else but in boiling water, making tea, and sipping it.

— Tea Master
Sen no Rikyu

Daniel R. Blume

the way is ordinary

Although everything has Buddha nature, we love flowers and we do not care for weeds.... A flower falls, even though we love it, and a weed grows, even though we do not love it.

— Dogen-zenji

Buddhists never hate what's ugly or love what's beautiful, because such absolutes don't exist in a continuous world. If the entire universe is one's own true self — heaven, earth and humans all stemming from the same root — the natural order includes things that are beautiful and ugly, sweet and bitter, happy and sad. Buddhists love all aspects of life and everything in between. Seeing this way makes imperfection, decay and death easier to accept — and life easier to live.

drawn-out rituals. Tea practitioners are accomplished in the arts of flowers, fine cuisine and — most importantly — etiquette and hospitality. During tea ceremony, a poem is read, a scroll is unveiled and the bamboo tea scoop is given a poetic name. The season is deeply honored in everything from the food to the pottery, and Sen no Rikyu's canons are revisited. For that alone, everyone should attend at least one tea ceremony.

Rikyu's four principles of tea — harmony (*wa*), respect (*kei*), purity (*sei*) and tranquility (*jaku*) — are the means to any good life. "Give those with whom you find yourself every consideration" has been a primary tea tenet since Rikyu's *wabi* tea style took hold, in a medieval society rife with warfare. In Rikyu's tea house — and in tea houses across Japan — samurai set aside their rank and swords and bowed humbly upon entering the tea room. Inside, they were equals. *Nanboroku*, one of the oldest and most important tea textbooks, said: "In this thatched hut there ought not to be a speck of dust of any kind; both master and visitors are expected to be on terms of absolute

surrender

Believing that tea tools chosen by Japan's foremost tea master would elevate his status, a poor tea practitioner from the country sent Sen no Rikyu all of his money and asked him to purchase some utensils for him. He was highly disappointed when Rikyu spent all the money on white cloths. When he complained, Rikyu said, "In the wabi style of Tea, even though one owns nothing, if one has only a clean white cloth for wiping the bowl, one is able to drink tea."

sincerity; no ordinary measures of proportion or etiquette or conventionalism are to be followed. A fire is made, water is boiled, and tea is served; this is all that is needed here, no other worldly considerations are to intrude."

"Tea brings people together in a non-threatening place to escape the modern world; then they can go back out and take that with them," Gary Cadwallader, an American-born tea master who teaches Rikyu's wabi style of tea at the Urasenke Center in Kyoto, explained to me. Tea masters teach that every meeting is a once-in-a-lifetime occasion to enjoy good company, beautiful art and a cup of tea. (This is known as *ichigo, ichie*, "once in a lifetime.") "If a friend visits you, make him tea, wish him welcome warmly with hospitality," Rikyu's predecessor, Jo-o, wrote. "Set some flowers and make him feel comfortable."

This hospitality endures in Japan today, in the common phrase *shaza kissa*, "Well, sit down and have some tea." It's a phrase that can change everything. A cup of tea makes everyone a friend.

the ten virtues
of tea

When Zen priest Eisai brought tea seeds from China to Japan in the 12th century. He also imparted its ten virtues.

1. It has the blessing of all deities.

2. It promotes filial piety.

3. It drives away evil spirits.

4. It banishes drowsiness.

5. It keeps the five internal organs in harmony.

6. It wards off disease.

7. It strengthens friendship.

8. It disciplines body and mind.

9. It destroys all passions.

10. It gives a peaceful death.

sen no rikyu's
seven rules of tea

1. Arrange the flowers as they are in the fields.

2. Lay the charcoal so it boils the water.

3. Create a cool feeling in summer.

4. Make sure the guests are warm in winter.

5. Be sure everything is ready ahead of time
   and do not fall behind.

6. Be prepared for rain even if it is not raining.

7. Always be mindful of the guests. (They're
   your first, your last, your everything.)

Carl Wycoff

Beadings, mouldings, and cornices which are merely for fancy may not be made by believers.

— Shaker Holy Orders, 1841

CHAPTER 3

feeling its influence: wabi-sabi through time

Wabi-sabi has infused Western design for centuries — though its advocates rarely knew it. It's in the plain, efficient homes built by the utopian Shakers (antithesis to the luxurious Georgian houses being built as the United States got wealthier) and in the simple, unsentimental Arts and Crafts style of William Morris and Gustav Stickley (a reaction to Victorian repression and the Industrial Revolution's isolation).

In the early 20th century, Frank Lloyd Wright's Prairie homes opened Westerners' eyes to the beauty of unadorned, streamlined rooms, "backgrounds for the life within their walls." As Wright's fame grew in North America, the Bauhaus movement's sleek steel and glass geometric design was taking hold in Germany. Closely tied to the International Style, this technological celebration inspired French architect Le Corbusier to create homes that he called "machines for living." Bauhaus prevailed mainly in intellectual circles — the general

It is common now to hear people say of such and such a piece of country or suburb: 'Ah! It was so beautiful a year or so ago, but it has been quite spoilt by the building.' Forty years back the building would have been looked on as a vast improvement; now we have grown conscious of the hideousness we are creating, and we go on creating it.

— William Morris

public never took to living and working in cold, steel-and-glass buildings — and paved the way for Minimalism to take hold in the 1960s. That spare, lean style, influenced by traditional Japanese architecture and epitomized by architect Mies van der Rohe's famous "less is more" motto, endures to this day.

The telegraph, railroads and steam power were accelerating everything, and stuffy, brocaded Victorian parlors signaled wealth and status when William Morris began his campaign for a return to handmade quality and the death of inessential decoration. Morris — a socialist whose naturally dyed, hand-printed wallpapers were, ironically, cherished by the robber barons — railed publicly and prolifically against the "swinish luxury of the rich," ornamental excess ("gaudy gilt furniture writhing under a sense of its own horror and ugliness") and the poverty of people who lacked creativity. "Have nothing in your home that you do not know to be useful or believe to be beautiful," he said, in one of the most often-repeated lines in home decorating.

Morris urged his students and disciples to constantly seek beauty in life's mundane details. "For if a man cannot find the noblest motives for his art in such simple daily things as a woman drawing water from the well or a man leaning with his scythe, he will not find them anywhere at all," he said. "What you do love are your own men and women, your own flowers and fields, your own hills and mountains, and these are what your art should represent to you." Saying that a well-shaped bread loaf and a beautifully laid table were works of art as great as the day's revered masterpieces, Morris's successor as the Arts and Crafts leader, W. R. Lethaby, said that modern society was "too concerned with notions of genius and great performers to appreciate common things of life designed and executed by common people."

As the leading spokesman for the American Craftsman movement, which evolved from England's Arts and Crafts, Gustav Stickley brought simple, solidly made furniture to the American masses at the end of the 19th century. Stickley employed "only those forms and materials which make for simplicity, individuality, and dignity of effect." He and his family lived in a simple log cabin, of which he wrote: "First, there is the bare beauty of the logs themselves with their long lines and firm curves. Then there is the open charm felt of the structural features which are not hidden under plaster and ornament, but are clearly revealed, a charm felt in Japanese architecture."

In the 1960s, the crisp, understated (Shaker-like) Danish furniture made by Hans Wegner, Borge Mogensen and Arne Jacobsen delighted the design world. Danish modern furniture, finished only with a sandpaper rubdown or linseed oil and embellished sparingly with natural materials such as leather, cotton and linen, was a breath of fresh air in an environment cluttered with all the new plastics and vinyls. At the same time, Charles and Ray Eames combined Shaker simplicity and innovation with modern industry to mass-produce furniture with

This excess of decoration might be called the "American disease." But let us hope that it has nearly run its course, and that we are learning to have beauty only where it is needed and appropriate.

— homekeeping expert
  Emma Hewitt, 1889

shaker sabi

When Japanese architect Tadao Ando first visited the United States in the 1970s, he wrote home about Shaker furniture. He admired its extreme simplicity and reserve, which he said exerted a restraining and ordering effect on the surroundings (high praise from a man who designs the surroundings). "Technically, the furniture was rationally made with no waste of any kind," he wrote. "In the great diversity of modern times, to experience objects representing an extreme simplification of life and form was very refreshing."

integrity. (Herman Miller has been reproducing the Eames's molded plywood and leather "potato chip" lounge chair, described as having "the warm, receptive look of a well-used first baseman's mitt," since 1956.) The Knoll furniture company began distributing Pennsylvania craftsman George Nakashima's polished cherrywood tables and softly geometric chairs. A softer, more human minimalism had been born.

In 1960, *House Beautiful* magazine editor Elizabeth Gordon gave a name to the spare, restrained style: *shibui*. Referred to variously as "the cultivation of the little" or "the cult of the subdued," *shibui* is the ancient Japanese art of not too much, of quiet grace through economy of means. The ancient Japanese character for *shibui* referred to water blockage, a symbol of restraint. *Shibui* colors are subdued (black, slate, dark brown and moss green), and *shibuimono* ("*shibui* things") have a nonmechanistic, timeless beauty, more than just pretty.

Two special issues that deciphered this Japanese concept of "severe good taste" and "superb understatement" — "Discover Shibui: The Word for the Highest Level in Beauty" (August 1960) and "How to Be Shibui with American Things" (September 1960) — sold out immediately. "*House Beautiful* has never had so deep a response to an issue from so many people," Gordon wrote at the time.

> *The Babel of modern color, which artists can regard less as a miracle of science than as a phenomenon of culture, is something that many artists have wanted to keep at arm's length.*
>
> — Jed Perl

western shibuimono

To help Americans understand *shibui*, *House Beautiful* developed this list of *shibui* things in 1960.

- Early American cupboards, chests and trestle tables
- 8th-century captain's chests
- Oaxacan black clay jars
- Shaker furniture
- Danish furniture
- 18th-century pewter
- salt-glaze pottery

George Nakashima's spare, simple furniture became popular in the mid-20th century.

kevinizing

Bucks County, Pennsylvania, craftsman George Nakashima's furniture was museum quality, but he refused to treat it as precious. "A certain amount of scratching and denting adds character to a piece. (In the trade, surface marring is called *distressing*; in our family it's 'Kevinizing,' after our son who could, when young, 'antique' furniture in record time)," Nakashima wrote in *The Soul of a Tree*. "To me, there is nothing quite so uninteresting as a shining, perfectly smooth surface that looks as though it has never been used."

Meshing perfectly with the era's spare, modern style, *shibui* had its moment in post-World War II United States. Baker developed a furniture line, Shumacher promoted *shibui* fabrics, and Martin Seymour called its line of muted, tasteful paints *shibui*. Erwin Lambeth Company built a Shibui House with burlap-covered walls, a fireplace textured with sandpaper, and Danish modern furniture. "Shibui has no bounds," said Erwin Lambeth president Kay Lambeth. "It's the unrestrained, the unobvious, the elegant in any culture — and we've borrowed ideas from the whole world."

six principles of slow design

1. **Reveal:** Uncover spaces and experiences in everyday life that are often missed or forgotten.

2. **Expand:** Think beyond perceived functionality, physical attributes and lifespans to consider artifacts' real and potential "expressions."

3. **Reflect:** Induce contemplation and "reflective consumption."

4. **Engage:** Share, cooperate and collaborate in an "open source" design process.

5. **Participate:** Make everyone an active participant in the design process.

6. **Evolve:** Look beyond current needs and circumstances so that slow design processes and outcomes become positive change agents.

Carlo Petrini founded Slow Food, an international organization that links food's pleasures with community and the environment, to fight the corporate banality that was destroying the culinary experience. Slow Food has spawned a Slow movement that includes Slow Cities, promoting local community, and Slow Planet, fighting the need for hurry. Slow Design, founded in 2006 by Carolyn F. Strauss and Alastair Fuad-Luke, aims to slow down the metabolism of people, resources and flows.

"Even today's new housing is informed by and designed within a vision driven by short-term economic goals," Fuad-Luke writes. "The offspring of this design paradigm are billions of products and buildings, most destined to lead very short lives in order to stimulate (replacement) production. This roller coaster of production is partly driven by an unswerving belief in economic growth as a given cultural good."

The parking lots and aisles of discount stores may be where the restless dead of a commodity civilization will tread out their numberless days.

— Lewis Hyde

slow design

Slow Design's manifesto urges designers to "satisfy real needs rather than transient fashionable or market-driven needs" by

- creating moments to savor and enjoy the (human) senses
- designing for space to think, react, dream and muse
- designing for people first, commercialization second
- balancing the local with the global and the social with the environmental
- demystifying and democratizing design by reawakening individual's own design potential
- catalyzing social transformation toward a less materialistic way of living.

california wabi

Charles and Ray Eames's enduring furniture designs were fresh air for many Americans in the mid 20th century (and beyond), who wanted a contemporary look but found extreme modernism cold and sterile. The husband-and-wife team used newly emerging industrial materials such as molded plywood and plastic to produce items for everyday use that were both beautiful and affordable. Sir Terence Conran calls their furniture "intensely human, charming, and kind." In a 1996 tribute, designer Tibor Kalman said the Eames's ubiquitous, unpretentious molded plywood "potato chip" chair was like a lover. "It can be lived with, seen every day, change and evolve, and slowly reveal its beauty," he wrote. Craig Hodgetts, who designed a Los Angeles exhibition on Charles and Ray Eames, points out that what the designers left out of their designs — "the pomposity, hierarchy, and stodginess associated with 'important stuff'" — is just as crucial as what they put into them.

The Eames's Pacific Palisades home, one of the *Art & Architecture* magazine-sponsored Case Study houses built in the late 1940s, demonstrated the freedom that can be found in straightforward, unpretentious design. Built with the same simple, clean lines as their furniture, the Eames's open-plan home was modern yet human, with a Japanese influence that included vertical-louvered blinds, tatami mats and Isamu Noguchi paper lanterns. It had a humble, fleeting quality, with a large, unbroken area where items they collected — driftwood, sculptures, mobiles, plants — could be brought in or taken away. Their living room was home to a continually changing collage of Indian embroideries, Mexican clay dolls, ceramic bowls, antique toys (which they collected as fine examples of design principles) and dried desert weeds — all treated with equal regard.

The Eames's often-stated goal was to help people see beauty in everyday objects. Charles Eames's grandson, Eames Demetrios, recalls spending hours following his grandfather around as he took pictures of cobwebs because Charles preferred spiders and picnics to museums or galleries for his grandson's art appreciation lessons. Rolf Fehlbaum, a longtime friend of the Eameses, said the couple had so much fun in their daily lives that they never took holidays. "They didn't need them," he said, "they enjoyed themselves so much."

Photo courtesy of Herman Miller.

modern tea master

Los Angeles video editor Joe "Guisepi" Spadafora began cooking his dinner and boiling a pot of tea on the tailgate of his truck, parked on Hollywood Boulevard, in 2006. He offered a little food and a lot of tea to anyone hungry for sustenance and conversation. "This small offering was enough to create friendships between all classes and colors, spark conversations on hundreds of topics, put a human face on those involved, and create a strong community out of a mish mash of people and cultures right there on the pavement," Guisepi writes. "Whether there was a Japanese tourist or a tattooed gangster with a shopkeeper or a Nazi punk, everyone related, everyone was comfortable sitting at the same level drinking the same warm beverage." Free Tea Party was born.

In 2008 Guisepi traded in his truck for a 1989 Ford/Thomas bus, which he has since remodeled inside, using salvaged wood. Edna Lu, as his tea bus is known, has a full kitchen with running water, benches with storage, a closet, a wood stove and a solar panel. Guisepi and Edna Lu travel the West Coast to cultivate community and encourage dialogue about peace, environment and health by serving free cups of tea to people on city streets, at parks and at festivals. "Tea provides a relaxing, warm atmosphere for people to be themselves and comfortably share with others," Guisepi states. Thousands of conversations between people who otherwise might not have met have been sparked during Guisepi's gatherings.

"The free tea concept is based on the idea that goods or services can be offered without expecting anything in return," Guisepi says. "This is known as the gift economy. We believe that selfishness should be balanced out by selflessness."

Guisepi says that free tea parties, though unique in the West, happen all over the world, every day. "Head to England for afternoon tea, South America for a Mate session, or any part of Asia for, well, just about any occasion," he points out. "Tea to these tea cultures represents connecting with friends and strangers, relaxing and shedding outside worries, slowing down, settling disputes, finding beauty in simple things. We are just taking these aspects of tea and bringing them to the people of North America."

part 2 | cultivate

I enjoy taking my time with each dish, being fully aware of the dish, the water, and each movement of my hands.

— Thich Nhat Hanh

CHAPTER 4

S slow

IN OUR RUSH FOR CONVENIENCE, WE'VE MOTORIZED NEARLY EVERY household task. Before I'm even out of bed, I hear my partner grinding coffee beans in the electric grinder. I blow-dry my hair, brush with a sonic toothbrush, make breakfast smoothies in a blender, prepare dinner using a little electric chopper and load my dirty dishes in a dishwasher. The machines bark digital beeps when the coffee's ready or the dishes are clean, urging me to stop what I'm doing to drink or unload. All too often I jump to and obey the digital command (especially if I'm trying to write or meditate). Without these noisy conveniences, my life wouldn't work. But in addition to the cacophony they bring inside, they rob me of the opportunity to slow down and pay attention to what I'm doing.

The Amish understand this. Contrary to popular belief, this religious sect carefully weighs every new technology to determine whether it would truly enhance and improve their lives. In most cases, they've found that the tradeoff of expense, noise and planned obsolescence isn't worth the opportunity to be present with a task. They see work as an opportunity to serve God and their communities and deepen their ties with each other.

When I was growing up, my family had a dishwasher, and it was most efficient (and led to less fighting) for my sisters and I to divide up nights and each clean the kitchen alone. It was lonely. I hated when my sisters got to watch *Charlie's Angels* in the other room while I was stuck loading the machine. Doing the dishes at home wasn't anything like the Thanksgivings we spent at my grandmother's house, which had no dishwasher. I was very proud to be old enough to join the women in the kitchen as they divided into sudsers, rinsers and dryers. As the china passed from one hand to another, the conversations that didn't take place at the mixed-gender dinner table flowed. This female bonding was as much a part of Thanksgiving for me as my grandma's mincemeat pie — even if it wasn't sustainable in modern families. (If my sisters and I been forced to hand wash the dishes every night, we all would have missed *Charlie's Angels*.)

Modern conveniences have been invaluable in freeing women from housework so they could do great things, and they make it easier for working parents to feed their children. But every once in a while, we need to rebel against the machines. Hand a towel to your significant other (the person you most text with) and ask him to dry while you rinse. Have a real conversation. Take ten minutes to sweep the floor with a real broomcorn broom instead of filling your space with the vacuum's roar. Spend fifteen minutes outside, under the influence of fresh air and sunlight, pinning clothes to a line. Enjoy the lack of convenience. Enjoy things happening slowly.

accelerated expectations

Moore's Law, which originated in the computer industry, states that every 18 months computing power will double or the price will drop by half.

on the line

*If we all did things like hang out
our clothes, we could shut down
the nuclear industry.*

— Dr. Helen Caldicott

Spending a few minutes outside, hanging your clothing and linens to dry in the sun, is good for you and for your clothes. It prolongs your clothes' life, leaves sheets smelling crisp and fresh, saves energy and prevents pollution. Using clotheslines or drying racks consistently could save you more than $100 per year in energy bills and keep up to 1,000 pounds of carbon dioxide out of the atmosphere.

In too many communities, though, pinning your laundry to a line can make you an outlaw. Homeowners associations and landlords often forbid clotheslines, saying they're ugly, could cause injuries and lower property values. The nonprofit advocacy organization Project Laundry List (www.laundrylist.org), which promotes air-drying laundry as a simple, effective way to save energy, has worked with several states to pass "right to dry" legislation allowing everyone to air dry.

The effort is inspiring old and young alike to discover the clothesline's benefits. "I had forgotten how pleasing a simple chore like 'hanging out' or, for that matter, hanging *in*, in winter, can be," Vermont-based artist Sabra Field states on the Project Laundry List website. "Saving energy and money is a side benefit."

moving meditation

In Zen Buddhism *samu*, or manual labor, is viewed as an opportunity to quiet, deepen and energize our minds. In most Zen monasteries, mornings are spent sweeping, dusting, scrubbing and gardening. For thousands of years, writes Roshi Philip Kapleau in *The Three Pillars of Zen*, "manual labor has been an essential ingredient of Zen discipline."

Washing dishes by hand is an opportunity for meditation.

against the machine

In the early 1800s, led by a fictional leader known as King Ludd, angry craftsmen attacked English factories and smashed the mechanical looms they believed were usurping and destroying their way of life. The Luddites, as they became known, were unsuccessful in halting the Industrial Revolution's sweeping changes, and the movement eventually died out. Luddism emerged again in the 1970s, as computers and technology began to significantly change the way people work, act and think.

Today's neo-Luddites are often dismissed as technology haters, but their philosophy is more complex. Rather than blindly accepting the Internet and digital communication as a panacea, neo-Luddites examine the ethical, moral and social ramifications of technologies that also bring us 24-hour video surveillance, spy satellites, extended life support and faceless communication. They want society to value humans more than machines. For every high-tech move toward efficiency, neo-Luddites point out, we lose the opportunity to connect directly with other human beings. Interactions with bank tellers and store clerks can be accomplished quickly and anonymously online, and texting has reduced conversations to acronym trading.

Neo-Luddites such as Theodore Roszak believe that blind faith in technology's promise of ever-greater efficiency creates even greater inefficiencies. (If you've been through a hard drive crash or lost your Internet connection for more than 24 hours while on a tight deadline, you know what he's talking about.) In a *New York Times* article titled "Shakespeare Never Lost a Manuscript to a Computer Crash," Roszak wrote, "I'd like my students to ponder the fact that by the time they have located their style sheets and selected their fonts, Shakespeare was probably well into Act One, Scene One."

John Maeda, founder of MIT Media Lab's Simplicity Consortium, writes of waiting days to get a refill for his label printer before he realized he could just write on the file folder with a pen; firing up his computer to look up a word on dictionary.com but getting beat to the punch by someone who found it by flipping through a dictionary; and standing nervously in front of an audience when his computer wouldn't talk with the data projector before he remembered that he's better at presenting ideas without PowerPoint. "The disabling effect of technology can be humorous in retrospect," he writes in *The Laws of Simplicity*. "But sometimes I wonder if being a Blackberry-toting cyborg is all it's cracked up to be."

Rita Mezzela

I find that what your people need is not so much high imaginative art but that which hallows the vessels of everyday use.

— Oscar Wilde

You can cultivate appreciation by starting each day with coffee or tea in a beautiful, handcrafted mug.

vision

TEA STUDENTS HANDLE EVERY UTENSIL, FROM THE BAMBOO WATER scoop to the ceramic tea bowl, as if it were precious, with the respect they would give a rare antique. This fundamental tea lesson is the first step toward cultivating your *wabigukoro*, or wabi mind and heart.

Start with the container holding whatever you drink to start your day. If you're using plastic or a mug from a now-defunct mortgage company, stop. Don't start your day with thoughtless consumption and unintended messages. Treat yourself to pottery that feels solid and heavy in your hand. Admire your mug's shape, textures and colors every morning.

For twenty-two years, San Francisco-based tea master Christy Bartlett, who represents the family of Rikyu's descendants, has spent five minutes every morning admiring her tea bowl — and every morning she finds something new. Studying her tea bowl's colors, shape and weight has trained Christy to look thoughtfully at everything she uses every day. The slightest seasonal light change and fresh produce from the city's markets become works of art under her gaze. When she cooks, Christy meditates on the different shapes she's making as she cuts vegetables into long, narrow slices or chunky bits. "It's simple and perhaps simple-minded," she admits, "but sometimes we need to be that way. And the kitchen is a place where we can develop a sense of the combination of aesthetics and function, pay attention to the small moments of life. If you can find great beauty in the small moments, there's no greater gift you can find."

Over sushi in a Kyoto restaurant, former Texan Gary Cadwallader, who now teaches tea at the Urasenke Konnichian of Kyoto, told me that visiting museums and shopping with an eye for color, texture and patina (not just price) cultivates the tea master's eye. "You can get a grater for a few hundred yen or you can get a more expensive one of copper," Gary said. "But the copper one will last long enough for your great-grandchildren to use. If we use high-quality objects in our daily lives, our life itself becomes a sort of training. We come to use each tool with deep care and consideration as we do in tea. Then, the way a person lives makes tradition."

Honing our sense of subtle beauty has nothing to do with our household budget and everything to do with learning to appreciate. In the early 1960s, *House Beautiful* editor Elizabeth Gordon wrote, "If

Beauty should be quiet enough so you can take it or leave it.

— Elizabeth Gordon

food muse

Food brings beauty into your home. When you unload your groceries mindfully, you notice the buttery soft cheese, the fine white hairs protecting the carrot's flesh, the chunky shapes or fine lines of different pastas. Crisp spring greens, plump August tomatoes and golden fall pumpkins are your medium. When you toss deep, red tomatoes in a pale yellow bowl or march a line of tiny pumpkins down the middle of a long table, you're making food art.

flower muse

Designate a prominent place in your home to hold something living — or once living — that you've gathered from within a mile of where you live. In spring, when the world is crawling with fresh blooms, and in fall, when colors are crisp and crackling, this is a cakewalk. It's harder to be creative in summer, believe it or not; daylilies and daisies are so easy, and most of the trees and bushes sport monotonous green foliage. Winter offers the best wabi possibilities: dried grasses and seedpods and naked, sculptural twigs and branches.

Wabi-sabi flowers are arranged as you would find them in the field.

you can't find beauty — for free — when you are poor, you won't be likely to have it when you are rich...even though you may have bought and paid for it." Gordon urged her readers to look at everything with a "pure eye," letting go of all associations about its price, its age, its social context and its prestige value. "You have to wipe away all judgments made by others, and merely respond to the object as you do to those things in nature that are moving: trees, sunsets, clouds, mountains," she stated.

Most of us don't equate the sight of waving grasses in a field or the sun landing on the horizon with money (which brings up work, stress and all sorts of other distractions). Natural beauty is priceless. We can take in and appreciate a great view because we don't have any hope of owning it, and we can't manipulate it (positively or negatively) to match our will. We don't think we can improve on nature, so we witness it with the innocence of someone who's powerless. With our egos out of the way, we can simply observe. Nature is wabi-sabi's mistress.

natural color

Wash your walls with wabi-sabi color. Instead of synthetic paint in never-from-nature colors, use milk paint or natural paint, made from food-safe plants and minerals. Milk paint is made from milk protein (casein), pigments, lime and clay. Used for centuries, it gives a subtle, muted color wash that was common on 18th-century homes and barns. Natural or organically derived paints are made from essential oils, tree resins, beeswax and mineral pigments. Because they're derived from plants, natural pigment colors are more subtle — like nature's.

Take a walk. Walk slowly, and fully take it all in. Look at the broad horizons, then narrow your gaze to a pebble. Run your hand over a maple tree's rough bark and compare that to the smooth, paper-thin birch skin. Check out the irregularities in a piece of limestone. Feel the light change as a cloud moves over the sun. Notice how weather and age create irregularity and distortion. The sun burns deep striations; the wind mottles; the rain rusts. Note the color combinations, how they graduate into one another, the ratio of strong color to paler, more-washed hues.

Walk in every season. Try to find contentment in winter's dim afternoons as deep as you find in June's exuberance. You have to try a little harder to find the beauty in November's pale, low light and barren fields, but consider how garish a blooming rosebush would be against autumnal muddy browns. Feel the earth signaling it's time to go within. After summertime's manic energy, appreciate the relief. (Rolling with the seasons should mean we get long winter naps like the oaks and the maples — even the bees. They're delicious.)

Japanese tradition holds that bright colors tire the eye — which then tires the body and soul. Wabi-sabi borrows its hues from late autumn: soft slate grays and matte golds, with occasional spots of rust breaking the subtle spectrum. In the absence of spring and summer's brilliant color palette — in autumn's soft, low light — these colors allow the eye to relax.

Wabi-sabi is sinewy, flecked browns and yellowed greens, the myriad stone and moss shades, a slate-gray cloud's washed violet underside. Like nature, wabi-sabi paints in multidimensional swatches that are never what they appear to be. A gray stone slab, close up, is speckled with crystalline bits, ranging from deep and dark to almost white, with orange and red washed gracefully into the larger scheme of quiet, recessive color. You have to look closely and carefully, and you still might not find all the colors that make up the monolith. Seeing color this way will also teach you to see.

Be rather restrained than over-luxurious in color, or you weary the eye.

— William Morris

Understated beauty becomes magnificent in natural light.

how to see

In 1940, Soetsu Yanagi, who founded the Folk Craft Museum in Tokyo, laid out guidelines to help people change their way of seeing and understanding beauty — by trusting their own intuition.

1. Put aside the desire to judge immediately; acquire the habit of just looking.
2. Do not treat the object as an object for the intellect.
3. Just be ready to receive, passively, without interposing yourself. If you can void your mind of all intellectualization, like a clear mirror that simply reflects, all the better. This nonconceptualization — the Zen state of *mushin* ("no mind") — may seem to represent a negative attitude, but from it springs the true ability to contact things directly and positively.

four ways to see differently

1. Give yourself five minutes of quiet time each day. (Great if you can meditate, but you don't have to. Just sitting on the porch is nice.) If you like it, work up to twenty minutes, adding a minute to each sitting.

2. Visit flea markets and junk shops without the intention of buying anything. Just walk around and note what you like. (If you see something you *must* have, take it home — the beauty and challenge of flea markets is that it might not be there tomorrow.)

3. Take a daily or weekly walk outdoors. Keep a mental or actual log of seasonal changes (color, light and nature's mood). To make yourself do this, get a dog who must be walked.

4. Create a treasure alcove. Place something you love (whether an heirloom or a stone picked up yesterday) in a special place. Replace it every season, then every month, and eventually every day.

My life is worthwhile even if I burn all the cookies. The creative process for me is like a path of discovery, so mostly my emotions through it are wonder and curiosity.

— Church of Craft co-founder Callie Jannoff

Making things yourself is personally and ethically satisfying.

craft

MAKING AND GROWING THINGS YOURSELF IS SOLID WABI-SABI — and a gentle rebellion against a globalized, mass-produced world. People make things because they love the process and for all sorts of other reasons from the political (exploitation and sweatshop labor) to the practical (a lot of the stuff we buy these days just isn't well made). We no longer have to make what we need to get by day by day, but for many the desire lingers — and even surges as a strong cultural movement from time to time.

Interest in craft cycles through modern culture. Traditional domestic crafts such as basketmaking and weaving, practiced by males and females alike, were crucial to pre-industrial cultures. In the 19th century, traditionally female chores such as spinning, weaving and sockmaking were taken over by males, who formed professional guilds to protect their livelihoods. Factory-run power looms, which could spin and weave faster and cheaper than the guilders and without any skilled labor, killed the cottage industries — and the domestic arts became a female hobby.

The Arts and Crafts movement in the early 20th century protested the industrialists' monotony with a call for a return to handmade furnishings, as the Colonial Revival movement's popular stitching and crafting societies brought many women back to handicrafts their grandmothers had left behind. Popular interest in traditional crafts faded out again until Alexander Girard, Dorothy Liebes and Jim Thompson led a revival of interest in the 1950s, and Girard began amassing the anonymous folk crafts collection that became Santa Fe's Museum of International Folk Art. In Japan at the same time, art critic and collector Soetsu Yanagi and potters Shoji Hamada and Kanjiro Kawai formed the Japanese Craft Society. Along with their friend, British potter Bernard Leach, they spearheaded an interest in traditional, handmade crafts that mirrored what was happening on the other side of the world. Yanagi's Japan Folk Craft Museum (a must-see if you're in Tokyo) houses "the arts of the people, returned to the people."

Today, interest in domestic arts such as knitting and sewing has risen as TV shows such as "Project Runway" have introduced young fashionistas to sewing, and knitting needles have become Julia Roberts' noted accessory. Trendicators call knitting "the Nintendo of the 21st century." I don't quite see it, although the Craft Yarn Council of

paint your own

Don't be embarrassed just because there's a kid party going on at the next table. Paint-your-own pottery places are legitimate creative outlets for those who aren't quite ready for the pottery wheel, and unfinished furniture shops are a creative (and frugal) option for anyone who doesn't own a bandsaw. If you can't make your own dishes and desks from scratch, let someone else do the hard work and step in for the fun part — giving your cup or chair a little flair.

a wabi belle

Natalie "Alabama" Chanin's studio in Florence, Alabama, is a throwback to the quilting and sewing circles that were once a mainstay in the South. Using Depression-era techniques, artists at Alabama Chanin hand-stitch recycled scraps and organic cotton (grown in Texas and knit in South Carolina) into impeccable couture that hangs in museums and is sold at Barneys. Their highly esteemed work has rekindled national interest in the rich Southern textile traditions, a huge boost to a region left destitute by the demise of American mills. The only reason not to completely fall in love with Alabama Chanin's rich, rustic garments is that they're pricey — really pricey. She gets that.

If you can't afford to buy an Alabama Chanin original, she'll show you how to make it yourself (or you can pay someone in your community to do it). Her books, *Alabama Stitch Book* and *Alabama Studio Style*, share patterns and instructions for making her most popular couture items, and DIY kits sold on her website facilitate the process. In addition to garments, Alabama Chanin also sells kits to make decorative pillows, quilts and doilies.

That kind of generosity isn't the norm in fashion design, but Chanin's an advocate for open sourcing and also believes that people find more value in things they make themselves. After making her patterns, she says, "many people finally understood why our garments are worth so much."

Alabama Chanin's doily kits contain everything you need to make it yourself.

*Fortunately, people
are artists who know
it not — bootmakers
(the few left), gardeners
and basketmakers, and
all players of games.*

— W. R. Lethaby

America says that a new recruit joins the 38 million other knitters in America every minute. Knitting's popularity hasn't rivaled the iPod and never will — but a lot of people knit while they listen to iPods.

Of themselves, the arts of spinning wool, making pottery and weaving baskets aren't political. They're satisfying, as they end up in useful things, and they provide a tactile meditation almost impossible to find anywhere else. My friend Katrina tells me nothing calms her more than sitting down at her loom — it cures her worst cases of jitters and blues. Katrina also taught me that "coping knitting" could get me through stressful business trips or family visits. Knitting teacher and retired philosophy professor M. Joan Davis says knitting is soothing because it allows the knitter total control. "You pick the colors, the pattern. Every stitch is yours," she says. When you're focused on knitting, it's a lot easier to just listen and nod with detachment.

My former boss Linda Ligon, who published several magazines devoted to fiber arts, says the satisfaction she gets from weaving a long, simple warp is the antithesis of the drudgery she felt when she stuffed envelopes as a kid. Both require long periods of repetitive, monotonous movement, but weaving or knitting results in a permanent, unique product — a piece of immortality that transcends her life's finite particulars. Setting stitch upon stitch, slowly building something that no

*My former boss Linda Ligon dedicates a
well-organized room to her weaving.*

machine could make better (or at least, the same) satisfies our primal desire to make things.

I don't have Linda's fiber arts brilliance, but I know what she's talking about. I find the same thing when I tile. My friend Carlos Alves taught me how to make mosaics with broken tiles nearly two decades ago, when he needed help with an installation in New York and no one else was available. I graduated quickly from assisting with his projects to covering my own flower pots, then walls and floors, with shards of tile (and bits of mirror and whatever else I can find in the free bin at the local salvage yard). I mosaic tiled every available surface in my last house, and I've gone to town on the little back patio in my

Broken-tile mosaics are an imperfect art.

townhouse, with plans to take on the bathroom as soon as a time window opens up.

I like mosaicking because it requires no precision. You can make the broken tile pieces as big or as small as you like, and the spaces between them don't have to be uniform. One piece leads to another leads to another, and then you step back and admire how they all go together. Carlos was right — anyone can do it — although now that I'm older it's tough on the knees and the back. Because tiling truly doesn't take special skill, I can recruit any willing fool to help (and relieve my knees and back), and some of my best conversations have

three wabi-sabi things anyone can make

1. Collages. Collect bits and pieces that appeal to you: magazine clippings, dried flowers, pressed leaves, wrapping paper, cards. Keep it in a box, and when you're feeling creative, sort through and start combining it on paper. You might be amazed at what results.

2. An indoor rock garden. Whenever a pebble or small stone catches your fancy, pick it up and put it in your pocket. Place your stones in a small frame on your desk. Moving the rocks around is a great thing to do when you really don't feel like tackling the task at hand.

3. Herbal vinegar. Steeping your homegrown basil and tarragon in vinegar for two weeks is a pretty and practical way to preserve it — but only for a couple months. Herbal vinegars are a transient art form that's best consumed.

taken place while I've sat with friends, in-laws and family members as we work our ceramic shard puzzles. It's like a quilting bee, with broken tiles instead of fabric and trowels instead of needles.

My house in Boulder came with a crazy-making garden. By August, the lemon balm had run amok, the peony bush — never caged — was limp and trampled, and a virulent Japanese knotweed strain had bullied out the lawn. The garden, too big for a working mother, was a tangled reflection of my out-of-control life.

As the kids got older (and easier) and I learned more about Colorado's brutal growing season — hot, dry days, cold nights, snow in early September — I gave that garden my best shot. I put in seeds for plants that like this waterless climate: slightly weedy black-eyed Susans, columbine, lamb's ears. I dug up and transplanted roses and heat-loving yarrow from my neighbor's yard and welcomed a chokecherry that made its way down from the foothills. (That tree was better than anything I planted. It gave us delicate white blossoms in spring and brilliant red-orange leaves in the fall). The indigenous species took care of themselves and managed to look good — even in August — without a lot of care and attention. The hardest part of gardening was keeping them tamed. I never did get rid of the knotweed.

My garden was hardly a wabi-sabi masterpiece, but following the principal tenet of embracing nature and nurture's delicate balance made it manageable. The wabi-sabi garden doesn't demand an English garden's formal precision and prissy styling — but it's not overrun with lemon balm and knotweed. It's somewhere in the middle. Plants are chosen because they belong in that garden, in that climate, and they're allowed to strut their stuff if they're considerate of the plants around them. They dance naturally with and around the stones and pebbles used to create winding paths and delineations, the rusty iron gate beckoning entrance, the trellis teasing vines up its length. Both

Just cultivate delight. Enjoy the sensory pleasures of the garden. That's number one.

— Diane Ackerman

non-arrangement

If you fiddle this way and that with the flowers and consequently they wither, that will be no benefit. It is the same with a person's life.

— Sen Soshitsu XV

Wabi-sabi flowers (*chabana*) aren't arranged. They're placed, in their natural form, into unpretentious vessels.

Nagarie, a simple, austere style of arranging flowers that literally translates as "throw in," evolved alongside tea ceremony in the 16th century. This method requires no training or talent, but it does require humility, in admitting we can't improve on nature, and a willingness to observe without judging or meddling. (No problem, right?)

"It is just meaningless to employ readymade ideas when arranging flowers," Shogo Kariyazaki, Japan's most famous flower arranger, told the *Daily Yomiuri*. "Flowers are already complete in their natural beauty. You need to have originality and ingenuity when making beautiful arrangements with them… Arranging flowers can be compared to cooking: You can make tasty dishes once you are able to apply your own ideas to basic recipes."

Unlike *ikebana*, which has a litany of stringent, stylized rules about how to combine and arrange flowers, *chabana* ("tea flowers") has only one: strive for a simple, natural look. Wabi flowers are always seasonal, arranged to look as they do in the fields. Each stem gets room to breathe; they're never crowded into big, frothy mounds. Stems aren't cut down to create uniformity; no frogs or wires are used. Branches are never forced, and tulips bending in their final days are as welcome as sprightly daffodils.

Minimalism is key: One wild rose bud trumps a blowsy display of English roses. Pick a few chicory stems from between the sidewalk's cracks and let them settle into an old bottle. Work with single flowers and small, odd numbers. (That tired old design rule that sets three as the standard became the norm because it *works*.) Forget about flowers and use a solitary branch (bare in midwinter, budding in springtime) or a few tall grasses. Trade in crystal vases for humble containers: baskets, bamboo slices, hollowed gourds, old jars, a well-shaped bottle that held dessert wine. (Pretty old wabi-sabi bottles — ranging in price from $1 in parts of West Texas to $15 in Northern California — are prolific at pawn shops and flea markets.)

Wabi flowers are arranged without pretense.

plants and guests are encouraged to meander and explore, as long as they're considerate. A garden's paths may lead to nowhere, and the garden might be more beautiful in January than it is in June. (A stroll through the winter garden, with its sculptural bare branches, brittle seedpods, and stark, naked plants, is a way to cultivate wabi.)

Above all, the wabi-sabi garden is a place to meditate on nature's infinite and perfect imperfection. Anything that gets in the way of that (like knotweed) is not invited.

This wall was my first endeavor into plaster. I coaxed my whole family, and even the neighbors, into helping. It's not perfectly done. We mixed some batches of plaster a little thick. (We probably should have supervised nine-year-old Stacey more.) But I love this wall because in it I see my kids (much younger), delighted to be playing with sand, clay and water. I hear trowels scraping and smell dank, clean earth — memories of smushing goo onto the wall deep into the night with my then husband, Matt, and my neighbors Hermine and Jean-Charles. Hermine's areas are tidy, Jean-Charles' artistic and Matt's precise. Mine are crude, like the wall behind Janis Joplin on the "Pearl" album cover.

The plaster was more forgiving of inconsistencies than we were. I've since divorced and left this wall behind.

Clay plaster is a forgiving medium.

speaking in stone

Jill Nokes's garden wall in Austin's Hyde Park neighborhood is a public art project, an invitation to stop and talk awhile, and a community swap meet. Built at leaning height to attract leaners (who tend to talk), Jill's stone wall is encrusted with fossils, shells, religious medals and bits of old jewelry that she's collected for years. Near the wall's archway, guarded by cast-concrete angels, a New York City snow-globe with the Twin Towers still intact pays tribute to the tragedy that occurred just months before the wall was built. Jill built ledges into the wall so that neighbors can contribute to the wall's legends. An old pocket dictionary, and a small antique medicine bottle and a set of false teeth holding an old spoon have appeared and disappeared along the ledges. It gives people something to talk about. "Remember the false teeth?" old-timers say. Newcomers get to hear the story.

Now nearly ten years old, Jill's garden wall has taken on a life of its own, even inspiring other vernacular walls in public pocket parks and schools. "I love that kind of handmade contagious enterprise," Jill says. "The 'trinket swap' just keeps expanding — we leave little toys and knickknacks out there that the neighborhood kids take and also contribute to — just like the knot hole in the tree in front of Boo Radley's house."

Matthew Bice

Jill Nokes's garden wall has become a neighborhood gathering spot.

*Put your hands
to work and your
heart to God.*

— Shaker saying

cleanliness

AN ANCIENT TEA MASTER DESCRIBED *WABISUKI* (A TASTE FOR ALL things wabi) as "putting one's whole heart to cleaning and repeating it several times." The Dalai Lama says that cleansing your environment is a ritual means of cleansing your mind. Cleaning is a wabi practice; every time we sweep, dust or wash sheets, we're creating clean, sacred space. Moving a broom across the floor and wiping dishes are little opportunities for meditation. So, why don't we ever want to do these chores?

Maybe it's the way we do them — and what we do them with. It's tough to be mindful when you just want to stop using the Pledge so you can breathe again. There's nothing spiritual about fumes that make you swoon when you squeegee the shower. The first step to "whole heart" wabi cleaning is to trash the chemicals and use softer, gentler (and cheaper) cleaning agents. Baking soda, vinegar and lemon juice clean and shine; vinegar cuts grease and deodorizes; baking soda scours and removes smudges; and club soda works for windows. (I learned my favorite wabi-sabi cleaning trick from my ex-husband's aunt, Cha Cha Paulette, who learned it from her Polish mother. Using newspaper to clean the windows prevents streaking.)

Just as the Japanese finish off their dishes with three perfect strings of inky black seaweed, you can complete your housecleaning with little garnishes: Soak a cotton ball in vanilla and place it in your closet to freshen up your clothes; pour vinegar into a small bowl and place it on a high shelf to absorb kitchen odors. Add some lavender essential oil when you throw clothes into the washing machine. Iron the sheets with a little starch. (If you iron your sheets, this really does make the difference. Who gets to sleep on starched sheets anymore?)

It can be tempting to use wabi-sabi as an excuse for not making your bed or sweeping the floor (going for that imperfect statement), and I do see how an afternoon at the movies can be more important than cleaning the house. But we don't get to justify that by calling it wabi-sabi.

Wabi-sabi isn't shabby or dirty, messy or slovenly — it's never wabi-slobby. Well-worn things shine in settings where it's clear they harbor no bugs or grime. They've survived to bear time's marks because they've been so well cared for through the years. Even the most rare and expensive antiques will never play well in a house that's cluttered or dirty.

Cleanliness implies respect. Tea masters teach that even the poorest wabi tea person should always use fresh green bamboo utensils and new white cloths for wiping the tea bowl. In tea, the host's cleanliness is a clear indicator of his state of mind and his devotion to the Way of Tea. *Chanoyu Ichieshu*, a tea textbook published in 1956, advises guests to look into the host's toilet if they wish to understand his spiritual training.

Keeping immaculate homes is a means of asserting control in our little corner of this unpredictable world. War, famine and crime may be unstoppable, but mold and mildew aren't. Conversely, clutter and disarray generally signal chaos lurking somewhere close behind. Good

We attribute vulgar qualities to those who are content to live in ugly surroundings.

— Elsie de Wolfe,
A House in Good Taste

the wabi-sabi cleaning cupboard

Hydrogen peroxide to remove mold and disinfect

Club soda to clean and shine fixtures and windows

Vinegar to cut grease and lime deposits and soap buildup, deodorize toilet, remove film on floors

Baking soda to scour and remove smudges or scuffs

Lemon juice to remove grease and tarnish

Salt mixed with water to destroy bacteria

Baking soda with vinegar rinse for stainless steel

Olive oil to polish furniture (mix 3 parts oil to 1 part vinegar for a cleaner shine)

Baking soda and vinegar can clean just about anything.

housekeeping strikes a balance between vacuuming the landscape rocks and letting things pile up and fall to pieces. The older I get, the better I am at this. I make my bed every morning because I understand that a well-made bed, with the sheets tucked in, is one of life's good pleasures at the end of every day. I clean up my dishes after lunch so my partner can make dinner. My house is clean enough to be healthy and dirty enough to be happy. It's my little rebellion against the advertisements that tell me to measure my worth by my spotless floors and germ-free showers.

In the early 20th century, most Americans were a step away from profound poverty. A clean, healthy household was as much a symbol of upward mobility as a dirty, disheveled home belied disgrace. As advertising blossomed in the roaring '20s, housewives were bombarded with messages about how to keep their whites the whitest and their windows sparkling clean. In newspapers and magazines and on the radio, they were told that laundry was an expression of love and that properly cleaning the bathroom would protect their families from disease. Everybody wanted a good, clean home, and the pressure was on women to provide. That message grew more shrill as TV gave Mr. Clean a platform.

As early as the late 19th century, domestic doyenne Catherine E. Beecher was alarmed by the number of women she met who seemed to be overwhelmed by their domestic duties. She advised them to make a list of all the things that needed to be done, figure out what they just could not do, then strike those off the list. "You will have the comfort of feeling that in *some* respects you are as good a housekeeper as you can be," she wrote in *The American Woman's Home, or, Principles of Domestic Science*, published in 1869.

Christine Frederick, who popularized home economics in the early 20th century, also saw the toll that the impossibly high housekeeping standards took on American wives. Houses should not be run accord-

Learn to let go. That is the key to happiness.

— The Buddha

ing to "arbitrary standards, set up by friends or the community," she wrote in *Household Engineering: Scientific Management of the Home* in 1920. She advised that a woman should keep her home according to "whatever methods conduce to the efficient management of her particular home, regardless of tradition, or what is supposed to be the 'proper' way."

Remember the 100 shades of gray found in Japanese kimonos? The same holds true with our housekeeping standards — we can learn to define success on a continuum. Unless you have severe allergies, changing the sheets every nine or ten days instead of every seven is not going to kill you or your family members. A clean bathtub is important, but sanitizing it every day with toxic scrubs is just not necessary. In fact, breathing in those fumes every day can be much more damaging to your health than a few germs.

When we're stretched to the limit trying to keep the floor swept and the clutter contained, wabi-sabi can seem like a chore. That's when it's best to stop trying so hard and just appreciate our warm bed at the end of the day — whether it's made or not.

The result is not the point; it is the effort to improve ourselves that is valuable.

— Shunryu Suzuki

Giving yourself a quiet, designated meditation spot will motivate you to sit more often.

CHAPTER 8

solitude

I LIVE IN BOULDER, COLORADO, WHERE A LARGER THAN NORMAL percentage of the population meditates. Lots of people had suggested I do the same. (My boss suggested it again just the other day, after I'd dropped my cell phone in the dog's water bowl while trying to handle the dog food bag while having a conversation with my partner about who was going to run by the grocery store.) Back then, I thought I was much too busy to just *sit there doing nothing* for 20 minutes each day. I was a working mother. I traveled. I…I…I….

I had to give this meditation thing a try.

Zazen, or "sitting Zen," is the practice of sitting in lotus position (legs crisscrossed) with a straight spine and upright head, eyes slightly open, lowered and unfocused, emptying the mind of all thoughts and focusing all attention on the breath as it enters and leaves the body. Simple enough. I would just sit, for five minutes a day. I figured I had five minutes to spare, and I was sure I could make myself be still for five short minutes. Think of how fast five minutes goes by when you're late.

It was torture. I tried counting to ten and stopping when thoughts intruded; I labeled them "thinking" and let them go. I never got past three before I had to stop for a thought, and that rankled. I turned my meditation practice into a challenge — and that brought up all my competitive drive (not my prettiest part). I got weird. "I made it past two today," I would tell my friends, as if I were talking about my golf score. It really mattered to me that I be "good" at meditation — that I get past three. When I saw how silly I was, bringing my report-card mentality to something as unlinear as meditation, I began to understand this discipline's magic. I could see what I hadn't seen before. (I'm still working on somehow fixing it.)

"There is no particular way in true practice," Zen master Shunryu Suzuki writes in *Zen Mind, Beginner's Mind*. I took his advice and moved on to other mediation methods that didn't trigger my basest instincts. Now when I sit, I let myself get lost in a candle flame; I need something else to focus on. I ring a chime at the beginning and the end, and I burn Nag Champa, Indian incense made from champa flowers, sandalwood oil and spices, in the hand-carved incense burner that my friend Rachel brought me from Thailand. At the end of my meditation, I pull a Tarot card from the deck, just for fun and a little frivolous motivation. (A lot of little rituals help get me in the mood.)

a new day unscrolls

Grand tea master Sen Soshitsu, XV, told his students to roll up the scroll in their meditation spaces when they retired at night, "just as you would change into your nightclothes," and to place it in the alcove. "When you rise in the morning, you can hang the scroll again with refreshed feeling. Although it is the same scroll, this will bring out its freshness and the significance of hanging it in the alcove," he said.

sacred space

I would like you, even in this busy age and even though your house may be small, to set aside a space (although it may seem a wasteful use of space) to serve as a place where you can reflect upon yourself.

— Sen Soshitsu XV

If you're lucky, you can find a space in the attic or have a small spare bedroom that you could dedicate to solitude and meditation. If you live in tight quarters, designate a quiet corner in your bedroom or even living room as your meditation space. Unroll a rug or a mat when you want to meditate, concentrating on creating a sacred space and changing the room's atmosphere. Hang a piece of art that represents peace and spiritual abundance to you. Keep a small table in this corner for your incense, candles and other meditation tools. (If your "space" is in a public spot and you don't want everyone to see these things, find a table with a drawer, or store them in a pretty box on the table.)

You can keep your meditation space spare and lean or surround yourself with tools and inspiration. Meditating is more comfortable on a cushion or in a straight-back seat. You also might want to bring in candles; an incense burner; a photo or statue of someone who inspires you; meditation or poetry books; a plant or seasonal flowers; a picture of yourself in a relaxed, joyful state; bells or singing bowls or a stone or branch from one of your favorite natural hangouts. Buddhist altars generally include the five offerings to the deities: incense, flowers, water, sandalwood powder, and fruit or cooked rice. You can follow this tradition or create your own offerings. CDs or iPod downloads that ring chimes at the beginning and end of a designated meditation time can really help if you're a clock watcher.

I still can't sit long, and I honestly prefer to get my quiet time in by practicing yoga or walking the dog. Adopting a Catahoula who needs three walks a day was the best thing I ever did for my psyche. Even on days when I'm far too busy (which is most), I have to stop and get outside with Rug. I leave the cell phone at home and head for paths that I know won't be populated, where I can be quiet and grateful.

When I was growing up, my dad spent hours and hours carving sculptures and building fine furniture in his basement woodworking shop. He was a passionate artist, but his passion waned once all four kids were out of the house. Dad's shop was not only a work space but also a refuge from our family chaos and a place to work things out when he needed some thinking space.

Everyone should have such a place. Humans are territorial beings, and without our own foxholes we get bothered and unpredictable. Every once in a while we just need to be alone, really alone. In most family homes, though, kids get their own rooms (and sometimes playrooms besides), yet parents share their bedroom and den. (Man caves are a response to that unfulfilled need.) "We need privacy even when we're married, to maintain separate interests and identities; otherwise resentment builds," clinical psychologist Alvin Baraff explains.

In the past decade, separate bedrooms for married couples has become a trend in building and remodeling. Today nearly one in four couples sleep in separate bedrooms or beds, according to the National Sleep Foundation, and the National Association of Home Builders predicts that more than half of custom homes will have dual master bedrooms by 2015. "Not that we don't love each other," Barbara Tober, former chair of the Museum of Arts and Design, told *The New York Times*, "but at a certain point you just want your own room."

Whether it's functional, housing a loom or shelves of beads, or simply a retreat space, your room is the one place where you can do whatever you want (and nobody needs to know). If you have only one

Perchance the time will come when every house even will have not only its sleeping-rooms, and dining room, and talking room or parlor, but its thinking room also, and the architects will put it into their plans.

Let it be furnished and ornamented with whatever conduces to serious and creative thought.

— Henry David Thoreau

extra room in your house, curtain it down the middle so you and your spouse can each have a share. Even if you live alone, designate a space that's off limits to visitors.

Inside your space, you can display your favorite projects or inspiring art, keep a big messy bulletin board with scribbled quotes and magazine pictures, bring in that totally comfy armchair that's way too threadbare for public consumption (and have it all to yourself), paint the walls the dusty chocolate that your partner calls "drab." This is the room of no compromise. Always wanted to live in a genie bottle? Paint the room in jewel tones and stuff the perimeters with cushions. (So

Your meditation space can include any and all symbols that mean something to you.

a room of her own

Architect Sarah Susanka, whose *Not So Big House* books launched a movement in quality-over-quantity homebuilding, designed her house in St. Paul, Minnesota, according to her own rule that every room should serve several different needs to keep space requirements down. Her bathroom was also the dressing room, and her breakfast nook was tucked into a circulation space. Only one room served just one person and a very specific need: Sarah's meditation space in the attic.

Sarah agonized, at first, over whether to include this room, but her longing for a space where she could escape and perform her daily meditation rituals won out. Sarah tucked her meditation room into an attic dormer and painted the walls a deep, contemplative red. There, surrounded by her favorite books, candles and incense, she found strength to write and rewrite her first book, *The Not So Big House*, when the publisher kept sending it back and asking for changes. In that room she found the voice to write a book that has inspired people across the world to see that smaller is better in housing.

"If you make a place like this, with the intention to make time to use it," Sarah says, "wonderful things can happen."

Sarah Susanka, founder of the not-so-big-house movement, carved out a meditation space in her attic.

Christian Korab, Korab Photography

it's weird. No one else needs to see it.) Feel like writing on the walls, or lining them with pebbles or shells? Do it.

If this seems hedonistic, consider what it could do for your relationships. I live in a townhouse with my partner and two children, my desk (and entire office) in the middle of everything and a shared bedroom that's also a meditation space and man cave. My partner's and my most ridiculous squabbles erupt because we just can't step away when tension's building. We struggle to keep boundaries between work and home because my writing desk looks into his kitchen.

Pieter and I have stolen little corners to make our own; I have my table in the garden for morning coffee, and because he's a chef he can request the kitchen to himself (and get it). We both long for a room where we could shut the door and have adult time-outs, though. Those really seem to work for the kids.

It's not the
tragedies that
kill us, it's the
messes.

— Dorothy Parker

Rather than overstocking the bookshelves, give space a chance.

CHAPTER 9

S space

MODERN AMERICANS FACE MORE CHOICES IN ONE TRIP TO THE grocery store than our grandparents faced in their entire lifetimes. All that freedom of choice is reflected in most of our homes, littered with more furnishings and gadgets than we need or want. Stuff is a major impediment to becoming wabi, and it's one of the hardest ones to break through. Most of us have been programmed to acquire more, more and more from the time we could speak. It's how our economies roll. "We live in a world overflowing with our own productions, a world in which objects besiege us, suffocate us, and very often distance us from one another both physically and mentally," Italian designer Claudia Dona wrote in 1988. "They make us forget how to feel, to touch, to think."

Take a good look around your house. Chances are, you have more stuff than you need. Are you okay with having a TV in every room (how did that happen?) or the glass duck collection that got totally out of hand? Do you need those sweaters that might fit again some day or the wild-haired, legless Barbies languishing in their own messy Barbie houses? You know, deep down, that the clutter you've parked in your home is as destructive to your well being as the constant buzz of a nearby highway. The thought of actually doing something about, however, it is absolutely paralyzing.

Wabi-sabi gasps for breath in homes rife with gadgets (even if all of them work) and tchotchkes (even if all of them are beautiful). The wabi-sabi room doesn't have to be prison-like or monkish, completely without ornament or whimsy. It simply shouldn't be suffused with extraneous details. Clutter smudges clarity, both physically and meta-phorically. Things you're holding onto because they were expensive, because they were gifts from your mother-in-law, or because you might need them some day are all just getting in your way. In a wabi-sabi home, space and light are the most desirable ornaments.

A couple of years ago I gave a workshop called "Making Your Home Your Sanctuary" in New York City. Before we got under way, each of us talked about what we loved — and hated — about our homes. Almost every participant mentioned clutter as his or her number one obstacle to having a happy home. They knew it was messing with their serenity, but they felt powerless to do anything about it.

New Yorkers do live in smaller, more crowded spaces than most, but they're not alone in their addiction to clutter. During a photo shoot in rural northern California several years ago, I met Linda, who had built herself a stunning straw-bale home, meticulously designed to give her abundant space and sunlight. A playwright and artist, Linda had asked her architect to include a large office and studio in the back of the house, but when we scouted it for possible shots, we couldn't maneuver through the mess. Linda had set up her computer on an old desk that was falling apart. Shelves were littered with out-of-date phonebooks and files, and every corner was filled with boxes of assorted stuff. A beautiful heirloom table was shoved into the corner as a place to pile more clutter, and her sculpting table stuck out oddly in the middle of the room. We moved it all out of the way to stage a simple, nearly empty photograph in which the room's graceful curves

Grace fills empty spaces, but it can only enter where there is a void to receive it.

— Simone Weil

Keeping knickknacks and furnishings to a minimum makes a home feel spacious and welcoming.

and clean light were the stars. "Oh, my gosh," Linda sighed. "This is actually a really beautiful room. I never come in here, because it's all so overwhelming. I've been wondering how I'll ever finish my next play."

I talked Linda into dumping the broken desk, and together we moved out all of the files and boxes. Linda pulled the antique table from its corner and set up a workspace looking out into the empty room. "There was just too much stuff," she kept saying in amazement. "I've asked so many people how I could make this a nice room, and there was just too much stuff!" As she opened the antique table drawer for the first time since she'd moved in, she was delighted to find a collection of linen napkins she thought she'd lost.

We Westerners struggle mightily with stuff. Every year, books full of advice on uncluttering and organizing are published; websites and newspapers revisit the subject regularly. Nothing sells magazines better than cover blurbs promising to help readers unclutter.

According to the Self Storage Association, the average person owns four and a half tons of material goods, including clothing, accessories, appliances and furniture. Experts say that most of us have 25 percent

beautiful and useful

In tea ceremony, beauty is said to be seven parts function and three parts aesthetic; objects should look great, provoke emotion and be absolutely functional. This is *yo-no-bi*, or "the beauty of utility." A vase, with simple curves and sensuous glazing, displays fresh flowers. A ceramic bowl holds both tea and history, connecting modern-day students with Sen no Rikyu's traditions. Everything in the tea room is yo-no-bi.

more furniture and 75 percent more toys than we need. Professional organizer Julie Morgenstern asserts that we use only about 20 percent of what we own; the rest is simply clutter. "Tangible clutter is anything that creates stress because of its appearance, condition, location, arrangement, and/or quantity," states organizing expert Harriet Schechter. "Having too much of a good thing can create just as much clutter as keeping lots of not-so-good things."

"We live in a cluttered world," Dr. Jerrold Pollak, a Portsmouth, New Hampshire, psychologist who studies obsessive/compulsive behavior including excessive shopping, hoarding and collecting, said in the *Atlanta Journal-Constitution*. "We get more mail, we get more magazines, we have the opportunity to buy more things. One hundred years ago, you couldn't have bought 200 pairs of shoes if you wanted to. Now you can get that in an afternoon." We buy more stuff because we can.

"For the overwhelming majority of Americans, an important part of living the good life simply means 'more,'" trend watcher Daniel Yankelovich said back in 1979, just before big-box superstores overwhelmed the retail marketplace and trained shoppers to buy more (cheaper) stuff made overseas. Surrounding ourselves with material goods proves that we've made it and makes us feel safe. We show the world — and ourselves — who we are through what we amass, the souvenirs of foreign lands, the beacons of good taste. We assert we're fanciful by collecting *Wizard of Oz* memorabilia, intellectually curious through shelves of books, discerning by the art we choose.

In their study "The Meaning of Things: Domestic Symbols of the Self," sociologists Mihaly Csikszentmihalyi and Eugene Rochberg-Halton found that most people find more meaning in a battered toy, an old musical instrument or an heirloom quilt than they do in expensive appliances. They find extensions of themselves in these things, and they actually look to them as reflections of who they are and what

Every possession is a symbol of the self.

— Georg Simmel

they can become. We seek out and hold dear items that resonate with us because they act as symbols of ourselves. Our stuff is us.

An entire profession has grown out of our inability to deal with our stuff. The National Association of Professional Organizers represents a legion of superorganizers who charge anywhere from $25 to $125 an hour to help get your possessions under control. A brutally honest friend — one who's not afraid to tell you that something is ugly, outdated or simply too much — is a cheaper alternative, if you can find one.

Years ago my friend Hermine, who grew up on a barge in Europe and couldn't become a clutterer because she didn't even have a closet, helped me go through my storage spaces one by one. Hermine got me to see the ridiculousness of hanging onto outdated leather jackets because they were expensive (back in the '80s) and the ugly mirrored chandelier hanging in the garage (that I'd paid $500 for after my first divorce). She helped me part with the spare blender that I kept in

Gently but with undeniable will, divesting myself of the holds that would hold me.

— Walt Whitman

what would gandhi do?

In his 1936 treatise, "The Value of Voluntary Simplicity," Richard Gregg tells of a conversation he had with Mahatma Gandhi when he felt guilty about not being able to give up any of his treasured books. Gandhi advised him to hold onto the books because self-sacrifice and stern duty create unsatisfied needs that get in the way of true simplicity. "Only give up a thing when you want some other condition so much that the thing no longer has any attraction for you, or when it seems to interfere with that which is more greatly desired," he said.

the laundry room (just in case) and garbage bags full of outdated, soiled, ripped or simply neglected and dusty clothes (some that I'd been carrying around with me since high school).

The result was liberating. For the first time in years, I could walk into my storage shed (I literally had to stand outside and toss things in before), and I could find the hedge clippers (we had three pairs, because I could never locate them from one season to the next). We could park the car in the garage — something we hadn't been able to do in years — and our son could play inline hockey in all that empty space. I liked every single item of clothing in my closet, and I made a vow that for everything I brought in, I'd get rid of another.

Keeping up with Hermine's high standards takes vigilance, and I'm kind of glad that we've both moved away from the neighborhood we shared so she can't see the state of the closets in my new townhouse, where I don't have a garage to absorb excess. At least once a year, I channel Hermine and get serious about paring down my overstuffed closet (wondering every time how it raged so far out of control again when I'm following the get-rid-of-one-thing-when-bringing-in-another rule and why I still have so many clothes when I wear the same three or four things every day). I search to find good homes in my townhouse for the stuff in the box marked "Knickknacks," which is eating up precious storage space. I know I should get rid of the heavy wrought-iron candlesticks and the funky pink ash trays that never found a place in my new digs, but I always put them back in the box under the stairs. I need to invite Hermine for a cup of tea.

No junk!

— Frank Lloyd Wright

Wabi-sabi's complicated two-step of spacious but not stark, comforting but not cluttered, requires nurturing and refinement. Slowly, over time, you pare down your possessions. You might live for years with three candles, a lamp and a bowl on a side table, then one day realize that removing the candles lets the lamp's clean lines and the empty

uncluttering made easy

Uncluttering is common sense; there's no magic to it. All the experts offer the same basic advice, in one form or another. It goes like this:

- Don't try to unclutter your entire house at once. Start with a drawer or a shelf and move on to problem areas (such as the garage or the basement) once you've had some smaller success.
- Maintenance is key. Spend fifteen minutes per day cleaning up daily detritus before it becomes overwhelming.
- Take everything out of a drawer or closet and spread it out in front of you. You'll eliminate more and organize what's left more efficiently if you can see it all at once. (This also gives you a chance to clear out the dust and run a damp rag over the surface.)
- Mark four boxes or bags "Keep," "Give Away," "Throw Away," and "Hold for One Year." (The last one's for items you don't need or use but just can't bear to part with yet. If you haven't touched these things in a year, their time has come.)
- If in doubt, throw it out. Give it to Goodwill or any of the charitable organizations who send trucks around to collect it. Or give it away on craigslist. Nothing moves faster than the stuff in the "Free" listings.

- If you can't find a good home for something, it's time to say farewell.
- Get rid of two items every time you buy a new one.
- Keep like items with like: cups, baking goods, candles, etc.
- Allow only three items on each surface.
- Cover only about one-tenth of a table; use objects of differing sizes.
- Just say no to refrigerator magnets. They encourage clutter.
- Keep windowsills clear of knickknacks and potted plants.
- Keep clutter contained. Use baskets and bowls to collect mail, pens and pencils, loose change and all the other odds and ends that collect on counters and tabletops.
- Storage is key to containing clutter. Storage areas should make up at least ten percent of your home's total square footage and be placed so that you can store items where they're used. (If you can't get rid of the stuff, hide it well.)
- Furnishings that do double duty as storage help minimize clutter. A wicker chest holding blankets can serve as a coffee table in the TV room; a small chest of drawers makes a great end table.

bowl's possibility shine through. A hand-knit afghan may be useful on the sofa in winter months, but clutter during the summer. One day you may decide that you don't need all those cookbooks out on the counter after all. (How often do you make Thai food?)

If you're not ready to get rid of family heirlooms and art that you don't have space to display, follow the ancient Japanese practice of rotating precious items through a special alcove, or *tokonoma*, on a seasonal basis. Assuming you have the storage space, rotating knickknacks through storage is much less painful than giving away or selling them. Try to connect the items you bring out of storage to the season — get out your grandmother's milk glass vase for spring flowers and group candlesticks to bring in welcome light in winter. You can expand on this concept throughout the house: replace a heavy woolen comforter with a light linen blanket on your bed, display only one piece of the silver tea set at a time. Putting things away for a while makes them feel new when you pull them out again. Think about how much fun it is to unwrap the Christmas tree ornaments and hang them on the tree each year — and how ready you are, come January, to put them back into storage.

It's easier to create spacious, clutter-free rooms when you're starting from scratch. A simple color scheme, with light, cool colors such as pale greens and grays that blend easily into each other, unifies any

He who knows he has enough is rich.

— Lao-tzu

three simple storage rules

- Store items where they are used.
- Store items at convenient heights — light, small objects higher and heavy, bulky items lower.
- Store similar items together.

room and creates a sense of spaciousness. Cover floors with natural-fiber rugs in jute or sisal and windows with simple shades in hemp or bamboo, then judiciously add elements. Place the largest pieces, such as sofas and armoires, near the walls rather than out in the middle of the room so they don't act as room dividers, carving the space into small parcels.

Choose furnishings that sit up off the floors, exposing the floor space underneath. Banish loud, brightly upholstered pieces; keep textures and patterns subtle and simple (the kind of pattern that you have to look at closely to discover a pattern at all). Also look for pieces with simple lines and strong, uncomplicated forms: Parsons tables, Craftsman-style chairs, American primitive pieces. Resist the urge to

The more cultivated a person becomes, the more decoration disappears.

— Le Corbusier

As Japan's most revered tea master, Rikyu served under fierce warlord Toyotomi Hideyoshi, known for his ostentatious taste. Furious that he hadn't been invited to see Rikyu's famed morning glory garden — an abundant display that was talked about all across Japan — the emperor announced he would visit. When he arrived with his entourage, he was shocked and again furious to find Rikyu's morning glory garden in shambles, all the flowers uprooted.

Hideyoshi entered Rikyu's tea house and was humbled and honored to find one perfect morning glory — clearly the garden's most glorious specimen — in a clay pot. Rikyu's gift could not have proved his point about simple, singular beauty any more elegantly.

glory in one

fill every space in the room, and eliminate any items — footstools, plant stands, spare chairs — that aren't crucial to its comfort.

As you add each piece, stop to weigh its effect on the whole. How does it relate to the others? Are you starting to intrude upon the room's empty, silent spaces? These empty spaces are what the Japanese refer to as *ma*, the space between or the balance between objects — and they're crucial. You want your eye to travel without interruption through the room and, ideally, into the next space or outdoors. If your gaze bumps into something along the way, that something should be relocated.

taking inventory: three steps to clutter-free living

1. Every six months or so, pretend you're moving: Do you really want to haul out six boxes marked "miscellaneous stuff" or ask your friends to carry all those crates of books?

2. Weigh the value of each item you own in terms of the effort it takes to clean, maintain and (perhaps) move. Do you love it so much that it's all worth it? If so, keep it. If not — someone else might.

3. Before you buy anything new, ask yourself whether you can live without it. Walk away from it; if you find yourself pining in one month, go back and get it.

Ample storage keeps clutter tucked away.

O Great Spirit,
help me always…
to remember the
peace that may be
found in silence.

— Cherokee prayer

silence

I<small>N DESCRIBING HIS DAYS AT</small> W<small>ALDEN</small> P<small>OND</small>, H<small>ENRY</small> D<small>AVID</small> T<small>HOREAU</small> writes of summer mornings spent sitting in his sunny doorway until noon, "in undisturbed solitude and stillness, while the birds sang amid or flittered noiseless through the house, until by the sun falling in at my west window, or the noise of some traveler's wagon on the distant highway, I was reminded of the lapse of time."

Quaint. These days, half a day spent sitting in a doorway would cause enormous email pile-up, and we have to drive far, far into the country to find the kind of quiet that can be broken by birdsong and wagon wheels. We live fast, noisy lives, facilitated by loud machines. High-speed expressways roar through towns. Cell phone conversations are everywhere. Our homes are a symphony of digital beeps, from the coffeemaker to the dishwasher. We barely notice lawn mowers, chain saws and barking dogs, noises that would have made our ancestors jump and run.

Thunder was the loudest noise that rocked pre-industrial humans. Before internal combustion, roars and booms signaled danger, and our bodies still react to loud noises with a prehistoric adrenaline surge: our hearts pump harder, our blood pressure rises, our blood vessels

In the concert of nature, it is hard to keep in tune with oneself if one is out of tune with everything else.

— George Santayana

constrict. Living in a din of ringtones, mechanical humming, unrelenting music and iPods, it's no wonder we get a little stressed.

"Calling noise a nuisance is like calling smog an inconvenience," former U.S. Surgeon General William H. Stewart said in 1968. "Noise must be considered a hazard to the health of people everywhere." Endocrine, cardiovascular and immune systems can all suffer from chronic noise, and children from highly noisy households have been found to experience delayed language skills and increased anxiety. Noise disturbs sleep, affects emotional well-being and may contribute to heart disease and mental illness.

My first New York apartment was on the corner of 101st and Amsterdam, across from a playground and a housing project. The streets were alive, at all hours, with people hanging out, shooting off M-80s, playing music really loud and yelling, sometimes caustically, always profanely, in phrases that got tangled in my dreams. Eventually I got used to the noise (my mother on the other end of the phone never did), but I never felt calm and peaceful in that place, which was otherwise a scream of a deal with an exposed brick wall, big windows and three real rooms. Within six months, I moved to a tinier and more expensive place, on 46th Street, far from any playgrounds.

It's not easy to find stillness anywhere in New York — although Buddhist monks manage to do it at the Zen Center on Broadway. Cities are loud. That's both their charm and their tediousness, and we've been trying to control noise in them since civilization began. In 6000 BC the Sybarites banned blacksmiths and cabinetmakers, with their bang-bang-banging, from working in residential areas (the first zoning). Julius Caesar tried to ban speeding chariots over cobblestones because of the clamor they created. In medieval Europe, horse carriages and horseback riding were not allowed at night in some cities; straw was strewn on the streets to muffle the sound of hooves and wheels by day. (Inside well-to-do homes, thick tapestries and straw on the floors protected bluebloods from hawkers' and street musicians' eternal noise.)

Modern living has made urban noise a bigger problem than the Romans or the royals could have imagined. (Who could have predicted that in a modern version of straw and tapestries, Queen Elizabeth would ban cell phones from Buckingham Palace?) Over the past 15 years the noise level in major metropolitan areas has increased sixfold; urban noise doubles every eight to ten years. Noise complaints are by far the most prevalent that the New York Police Department's Quality of Life hotline receives. Noise is Americans' number one complaint about their neighborhoods and the most-cited reason for moving, according to the 2000 Census. "Background noise" from planes, car horns, voices and music in the typical urban home averages 50 to 60 decibels (about equal to the decibel level of an air conditioner in use).

Escaping to the country isn't much of an escape. Even in the unpopulated wilderness, where cell phones don't work and no one's found a way to pipe in Muzak, our engines roar overhead. In 1998 Gordon Hempton, a sound recordist attempting to build a natural sound library, toured 15 states west of the Mississippi and found only two areas — in the Colorado mountains and Minnesota's Boundary Waters — that were free of motors, aircraft, industrial clamor or gunfire for more than 15 minutes during daylight.

A few years ago, during a women's retreat in the Rocky Mountains, our leaders sent us all off in different directions with pencil and paper, to find a tranquil spot and record what we heard. "Airplane," I wrote. "Airplane. Airplane. Airplane. Helicopter." Then finally, blessedly, "Mosquito."

Our homes should be a refuge, a place where we can cultivate what the Quakers call the "still, small voice within." In today's homes, that voice has to get loud to be heard amid the constant bumps and

I try to listen to the still, small voice within but I can't hear it above the din.

— from *Little Audrey's Story*, by Eliza Ward

grinds inside our homes: refrigerators' and air conditioners' constant humming, the heater's low roar as it gears up, the startling thunk of the washing machine's automatic water shutoff, the coffee grinder's high-pitched whirr, the neighbor kid practicing his bass guitar or violin (sometimes it's hard to decide which is worse). With sonic technology, even our toothbrushes are loud.

Subdivisions full of large homes on small lots mean that neighbors' noise is our noise. Open floor plans, with rooms merging into one another through wide, doorless passageways or waist-high walls, allow sound to bounce freely around our houses. Great rooms connect everything to the kitchen — the loudest room in the house — making for afternoon cacophony when the kids are watching "SpongeBob" and Mom's running the food processor and the dishwasher.

Modern construction blocks sound much less than older buildings do. Most interior walls today have Sound Transmission Class ratings of about 30, a level at which loud speech can be heard through the wall. Gypsum board, the wallboard of choice since World War II, absorbs much less sound than the inch-thick plaster walls used in pre-war buildings. Old-fashioned cast iron pipes were denser, and so quieter, than today's plastic pipes.

Our homes ring with laughter, play, celebration, music (without which, Plato said, "the soul becomes feeble, deaf, and blind"), rain on the roof and the sparrow's song through the window. Just as Thoreau considered Sunday church bells "natural melody worth importing into the wilderness," these are sounds we welcome.

Sound quality is as important as the visual landscape, but Canadian musician R. Murray Schafer, who developed "acoustic ecology," asserts that in our eye culture, we've forgotten how to listen. He suggests fine-tuning your ears through "soundwalks," walking for about an hour at

The ears are the most intimate organs of the soul.

— Thomas Moore

different times of the year and listening to the seasons change: the robins' return, the autumn wind's whistle, the snow's crisp silence. When you return home, write down your experiences. Or keep a sound journal, a daily record of what you hear. Through this, your home's voices will emerge. At what time of day do planes fly over? Had you noticed how loud the grandfather clock ticks? Or how loud the dog snores? (That one can be hard to miss.)

The goal is to bring more good noise into your home and find ways to eliminate the bad. The first part's pretty easy: tickle your kids, tell more jokes, download some good music, play your piano, hang wind chimes. Just be careful. Too many wind chimes, or chimes that are too large for your space, will simply add to the din. Also consider placement. I gave my mom a fountain when she moved from the country into the city a few years ago. She set it up near her bed — for one sleepless night.

If your home is particularly loud — especially in the bedroom, home office or meditation space, where quiet is not a luxury but a priority — bring in a white noise generator. Small enough to fit into your palm, these devices produce gentle rushing sounds that help mask traffic noise and voices. (Pink noise generators are more intrusive, with ocean, rain and waterfall sounds.)

Acoustical perfume probably couldn't be considered wabi-sabi. But sometimes modern ingenuity is the only answer in a modern world.

Noise abatement ranks right up there with improving energy efficiency and designing products for reliability.

— Norman Remich,
Appliance Manufacturer

When my then husband and I ripped out the grimy carpet in our house and replaced it with hardwood floors, it was a huge improvement aesthetically and sanitarily. The smooth, golden wood was no longer a trap for dog hair and dust, and the whole family breathed easier. We hadn't counted on the difference in noise level, however. With nothing to absorb the impact of footsteps, paws and voices,

In the attitude of silence the soul finds the path in a clearer light, and what is elusive and deceptive resolves itself into crystal clearness.

— Mahatma Gandhi

everyone's every move echoed through the house in a way it hadn't before. (When I moved out of that house and into my townhouse, I replaced the carpet with cork.)

Carpet, for its many flaws, does a lot to muffle our homes' noise. Hardwood floors, for their many virtues, are big drumheads that send sound reverberating through a house. Bare walls (especially if they're plaster) and plain wood furniture do the same. You can minimize this by making sure that at least 25 percent of every room contains some absorbent material such as drapes, Venetian blinds, fabric wall hangings or large canvas paintings, or carpet. Book-filled bookcases and deep, squashy upholstered furniture — the softer and larger, the better — will also help stop sound from bouncing around the room.

If this sounds a bit Victorian, think about nubby hemp, rustic burlap or raw silk for draperies. Sisal, sea grass and cork can absorb sound underfoot. Burlap-covered homasote, a fiberboard made from recycled newspapers, is a terrific option for walls.

Soundproofing facilitates stillness, but quiet homes are the product of their makers. "I live on the Upper East Side," Arline Bronzaft, who has conducted several studies on how noise affects children, told me. "Do I have doubled-glazed windows? Yes. I'm not a fool. But what makes a home quiet is the people who live there."

epicurean listening

Less is more, and you can reduce slowly.

- Leave the television off for one night a week.
- Practice a few moments of silence before each meal.
- Turn off the radio during your morning commute.
- Make time in the afternoon for a quiet cup of tea.

Thick mohair Victorian-era curtains help block street noise.

put cork in it

In 1918, beleaguered by the din made by revelers on the street below his Paris apartment, Marcel Proust lined his entire bedroom with cork so he could complete *The Remembrance of Things Past* (a technique now referred to as "Prousting"). Cork is a great sound-absorbing material because 50 percent of its molecular structure is air; use it for floors and also to line the inside of cupboards and drawers, which will prevent clanging as you put away dishes and silverware.

Cork comes from cork oak bark, which can be harvested every nine to twelve years without harming the tree. Most cork flooring is made from the waste generated in making wine stoppers — meaning it's a post-industrial product made from a natural material. A naturally waxy substance in the bark repels fire, mold and mildew, and insects and termites.

When I moved into my townhouse a few years ago, I immediately replaced the carpet in my kids' rooms and the family room with cork flooring. Though I like carpet's warmth and noise-muffling qualities, I've never been a fan of it for health reasons. Even after all the chemicals used to manufacture and install it have outgassed, carpet is a noxious sink. All the dust, dirt, chemicals and other toxins that come into my home eventually settle in there, and it's impossible to keep wall-to-wall carpet truly clean. Cork floors make my kids' spaces feel cozy and nurturing, but they're tough enough that the dog is always welcome.

Cork is as durable as hardwood but softer and more forgiving. Melissa Clements, who owns Eco-Friendly Flooring in Madison, Wisconsin, convinced me to install it when she told me: "I have multiple chemical sensitivities and allergies, two dogs, a child with autism and asthma, and three kids under age six, so we're on the floor a lot. The cork floor provides a safe, useable space in our basement that will last forever. It's kid-friendly, animal-friendly and keeps the house free of VOCs, dander and dust. Plus, it's very warm, visually and texturally."

I bought cork planks, which click together to create a "floating floor" with a half-inch gap between the cork and the concrete that prevents moisture buildup (which could lead to mold). Made from formaldehyde-free, waterproof fiberboard covered with a layer of high-density cork and treated with acrylic finish, the interlocking planks don't require glue or nails, making them an easy DIY install (although I hired a guy who installed it in two afternoons).

I was lucky to have Melissa's help when I picked out my cork. As the material has become more popular in recent years, substandard cork has become a problem. Until a few years ago, virtually all cork flooring came from Europe, primarily Portugal and Spain, where manufacturing and emissions standards are higher than in the United States. Now cork flooring products are being made in China, where standards are more lax. When buying cork, always find out the country of origin — and go beyond the name. (Lisbon Cork is made in China). Get a sample and let it sit in the sun for an hour, then take a whiff. If you smell formaldehyde, don't buy it.

Arline has found that high academic achievers grow up in homes where TVs, stereos and computers don't blare and where quiet dinnertime gatherings (without cell phones) offer ample opportunity for conversation. "A noisy, cluttered home doesn't foster parent-child interaction," Arline said. "Yet we've created households that don't value and esteem quiet and serenity. This is important not just for mental health and learning, but for spirit and soul."

Silence can be scary (or worse, boring), so we fill it. Pandora radio and iPods let us control our sound environment at all times, keeping us out of that silent place where things can get uncomfortable. Arline says people turn on the television the minute they walk through the door and leave it on until they go to bed because "they're afraid to be in touch with themselves." I get that.

One November I went on a silent retreat at an abbey deep in the most barren, rocky part of northern Colorado. No kids, no email, no phone — nothing to distract me from meditating and writing. The nuns even gave us little signs to wear around our necks that said, "I am on silent retreat. Please don't talk to me." (A friend wanted to have T-shirts made.) The whole experience depressed and terrified me. The dark bore down cold and early, and I couldn't escape into the Gourds or Michael Franti when the writing (and thinking) got hard. I wanted to talk to my kids. I wrote bleak passages.

I woke up with the weak morning light and felt better than I'd felt in ages. All that had seemed so dismal the night before seemed faint and beatable. As I drove through the deep canyons toward Fort Collins and home, I kept the stereo off. I felt purged. I can't say I was happy, really, but I started to understand why the monk goes to the mountain. I felt calm.

soundproofing: the advanced course

The following noise-mitigation techniques rank from small, quick fixes to major projects. If you don't mind a little noise, you'll find more than enough satisfaction with the quick fixes. If you're highly sensitive to noise or live near an airport or a highway, across the street from a fire station or anywhere in New York City, you might want to take a closer look at the bigger projects. It's good to have options if the noise level starts getting to you.

Quick Fixes

- Place ½-inch thick rubber or cork pads under the legs or corners of large heavy appliances such as washing machines, dryers and refrigerators to stop vibrations from transferring to the floor.
- Move appliances at least two inches away from the wall.

- Place rubber pads under small appliances, dish racks, on countertops near the stove and in sink basins.
- Put stereo speakers on stands to prevent turning floors or walls into whole-house speakers. Alternatively, place rubber vibration isolator mats (available from office supply, computer or audio equipment stores) beneath speakers and printers.
- Install rubber or cork tile on the backs and shelves of cabinets.

Cracks and Crevices

Sealing any small opening through which air and noise can enter a room is the cheapest, fastest and most efficient way to block noise. (And it doesn't hurt your home's energy efficiency, either.) You can test for sound leaks by darkening a room to see where light — and therefore sound — is seeping in.

- Caulk or seal all cracks or openings in walls and doors.
- Seal holes around electrical service entrances, vents, steam or water pipes, and air conditioners — any gap where sound can sneak in.
- Remove the faceplates from electrical outlets and switches, and caulk the spaces between the box and the wall.
- Remove baseboards and seal the space between the walls and the floors with caulking compound.
- Remove recessed light fixtures from the ceiling, seal the holes with wall-board and spackling compound and replace with track or soffit lighting.

Doors

- Install storm doors.
- Replace hollow-core doors with solid doors. If that's not possible, add an extra surface of plywood to both sides of the door to help absorb more sound.
- Place weather stripping around all doors, even interior ones. Replace any weather stripping that's loose or admits light or air.
- Use flexible rubber threshold seals to close off the space below doors.
- Cover up the mail slot.

Windows

Windows are most often the weak points that allow sound into a home.

- Invest in double-glazed windows. They provide noticeably improved soundproofing because of the air cavity between the two panes.
- In really loud areas, consider double windows with a large air gap. Place acoustic absorbent material on the perimeter reveal around the gap.
- Caulk existing windows and equip them with gaskets to provide an airtight seal.
- Install storm windows with heavy glass and good weather stripping.
- Place shutters inside the window.

Insulation

- Line the cavities that hold the dishwasher, refrigerator and trash compactor with sound-absorbing materials.
- Insulate attic and walls.
- Add mass to walls with a second layer of drywall. Place the second layer as a "floating wall," apart from the first, to create an air space baffle. The thicker the space, the more effective the barrier will be.

Plumbing and Mechanical Systems

- Heavily insulate plastic pipes to minimize the gurgling and sloshing.
- Install water hammer arresters, available at hardware stores, to absorb the shock of copper pipes clunking when the washing machine or dishwasher valves quickly shut off the water supply. Whole-system hammer arresters can be soldered into the water line; individual appliance arresters simply screw on.

- Tune up the furnace: lubricate the blower, replace filters, check belts and pulleys for wear.

Landscaping

- Plant trees and hedges. At the very least, they provide psychological relief by blocking noise sources from view.
- Conifers and broadleaved evergreens are the most effective year-round noise blockers.
- Install a barrier wall or fence with a solid, continuous surface. It should be tall enough to hide the entire roadway from the house.
- Mask noise with fountains, waterfalls or tall ornamental grasses that make a soothing sound when the wind blows.
- Replace electric or motorized leaf blowers, lawn mowers and hedge trimmers with old-fashioned rakes, push mowers and clippers.

quieter appliances

Electric appliances such as refrigerators, dishwashers and washing machines bring noise into your home. Later-model, energy-efficient machines are also quieter, and you can shop with noise abatement in mind. (Miele claims that its vacuum cleaner is so quiet that you can talk on the phone while using it.)

Dishwashers

Newer dishwashers are much quieter than the machines of old, although the pumping and swishing that cleans the dishes can't be entirely silenced. Check the acoustics of the cabinetry and the floor when you install your dishwasher, and seriously consider models made by Bosch and Miele, companies that have made the most advancements in quiet machines. Thermador, Gaggenau, Maytag and GE also have models that make sound abatement a priority.

Refrigerators

Energy-efficiency standards implemented in 2001 mandated that all refrigerators use smaller compressors and inject foam into the door and side panels to increase insulation — which also muffles sound. The following models make sound abatement a priority:

- Thermador
- Viking ProChill Temperature Management System
- KitchenAid Whisper Quiet
- GE Quiet Package
- Amana SofSound II

Washers and Dryers

Now that laundry rooms have been elevated out of the basement (where it didn't matter if washers and dryers knocked around and gurgled loudly as they drained), quieter operation is a bigger priority. If your laundry room is upstairs next to the master bedroom, you'll want to pay especially close attention to noise abatement. The new front-loading, high-efficiency washers use less water and detergent — and therefore make less noise. Insulate the room's walls and make sure the washer and dryer are mounted on a strong, level surface so that their spinning vibrations don't cause them to shake and spin off-kilter.

Barbara Bourne

There is a cachet
now in dust. It
gives people a past
they haven't had.

— Min Hogg, editor,
World of Interiors

Embrace the rust.

CHAPTER 11

Wabi-sabi

WABI-SABI LURKS IN FLEA MARKETS, HIDDEN IN PILES OF MUSTY old junk. It takes a trained eye and hours of rifling through rusty hardware to find a piece with good history and character that also serves whatever need you're looking to fill. You have to be willing to stop in thrift and antique stores anywhere and everywhere (it helps if your traveling partner likes flea markets, too), and above all, you have to love the hunt. More often than not, you'll leave empty handed — but you will have spent a pleasant afternoon.

Flea market success requires agility, flexibility and dedication. There's an antique mall, thrift store or flea market of some sort in every city of any size across the United States. When you find one, it's good to be prepared.

- Make a plan to help guide your search, but don't be attached to it. Flea markets' beauty is their unpredictability, so go with an open mind. Be ready to scrap your plan based on what you find.
- Bring a list of items you want or need, along with specific sizes and room measurements.
- Know the market value of the items you're after. (You can find that online at kovels.com.)

Before beginning a Hunt, it is wise to ask someone what you are looking for before you begin looking for it.

— *Pooh's Little Instruction Book*, inspired by A. A. Milne

- Bring paint samples, fabric swatches and photos of the rooms you're decorating.
- Bring a tape measure, a notebook, tote bags and cash.
- Be prepared to haggle. Antique dealers and flea market sellers admit that a 20 percent price adjustment isn't unusual.
- The best selection happens early; the best bargains come at the end of the day.
- If you love it, buy it — but remember, most purchases are final.

Ten years ago, old barn siding and salvaged-wood flooring were the building industry's most prevalent examples of reuse. Vintage beams and joists were for boutique builders (and buyers) — far beyond most common folk's reach. Today, salvaged shutters, columns, bricks and fixtures are design staples. As the building industry has grown more conscious about demolition, and the Internet has made selling and finding materials much easier, quality parts from worn-out houses

mix and match

When decorating with flea market finds, you don't have to be a slave to each item's history. Mix and match Shaker with Midcentury Modern, American Primitive with Southwestern. All that really matters it that each item appeals to you. "The essence of this look is that it's a look for a lifetime," says Wendy Lubovich, a consultant for Dayton's Paris Flea Market in Minneapolis. "It's about finding a piece that you love. And you'll find that if you love everything in the room, it will somehow go together."

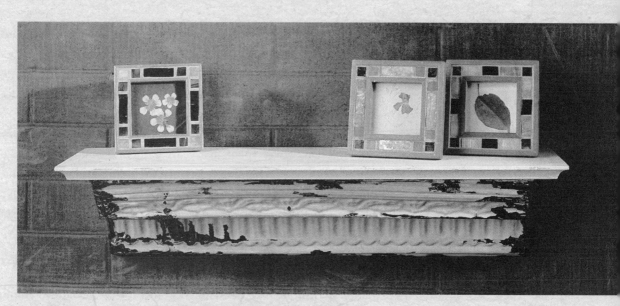

Smaller salvaged items such as this shelf bring history without a lot of hassle.

secondhand savvy

The beauty in flea market finds is that they don't have to be put to their original use.

- A lidless teapot becomes a flowerpot.
- An old window frame frames a mirror.
- Jelly jars hold spoons.
- Old picnic baskets make great side tables (and offer storage).
- Shawls and scarves hide stains in the sofa.
- A butter dish holds watches.

are becoming more widely available. Builders and homeowners are giving houses a little soul with antique doorknobs and radiator grates and saving money by using solid, old lumber a second time around. Building with salvage gives a new house depth and history it couldn't otherwise have.

Salvage brings soul — and stories. To build his family's home in Alabama, Guy Baker spent five years gathering building materials from every town in Randolph County, including lumber, trim and windowpanes from the county's oldest church. Glenda Alm built her 850-square-foot home in Oregon using Douglas fir boards, posts and beams salvaged from the dismantled Oakland Naval Base, where her father had been stationed. Casa Neverlandia in Austin, Texas, has Moroccan and Indian posts and lintels built into the fireplace mantel and the entryway — launch points for conversations about architect-designer owner James Talbot's adventures in faraway lands. In Berkeley, California, architect Karl Wanaselja spent countless Saturdays in automobile junk yards, finding just the right parts to finish off his renovated Victorian duplex. He collaged together a few different

indiana's stash

Inspired (at least in name) by Le Marche aux Puces, a Parisian market that sold flea-infested sofas, flea markets have become a huge business — and an important pastime — for Americans. In Indiana, 1,300 dealers line interlocking highways along Richmond's Antique Alley. Centerville, just six miles west, is said to hold more antiques per square capita than any other town in the United States.

basket case

This basket, one of dozens of items cluttering a table at the Tesuque, New Mexico, flea market, didn't look like anything special at first. It looked well-made, if rickety, but it lacked the glamour of the brightly beaded baskets beside it. Yet it called to me, so I picked it up for a closer look. It held a faint smell of smoke in its weave, and the tattered leather band around the edges spoke of much good use. The tiny cream-colored shells were uniform yet irregular, in shades of beige with the palest yellow centers, and they seemed to hold the vessel together. I imagined its maker stringing those tiny shells around the basket's perimeter, thought he'd be proud to know that despite all the knocking-about this basket had endured, not one shell was missing.

A flea market find, this basket is both useful and beautiful.

Pollution is just an untapped resource.

— Buckminster Fuller

Meghan and Aaron Powers built their home almost completely from recycled and salvaged materials.

truck tailgates to make a deck rail, and he hung a Mazda RX7 rear windshield over the back door as an awning. Determined to use some part from a Volvo, which he calls "the badge of Berkeley," Karl lined up two of the Swedish car's doors side by side to make a stair railing.

In Victor, Idaho, Meghan and Aaron Powers built their 836-square-foot home almost completely from materials they found in local landfills and demolition sites. They scoured their area's dumps — "about the only place we didn't look for stuff was the dead animal pit," Meghan said — and gathered appliances, doors, windows, floor tiles, garage doors, chimney pipe, granite countertops, corrugated steel ceiling and roofing, and lumber. Using salvage was the only way the couple, determined to avoid a construction loan, could afford to build a home — and it was an important part of their efforts to reduce their impact. "It hit us that the biggest way we could practice green building was first by reducing — figuring out how small a space we could realistically live in — and then finding as many ways to reuse materials as possible," Meghan said.

Meghan Powers

old soul

Since he founded Mountain Lumber in 1974, Willie Drake has rescued more than 20 million board feet of pine and other woods that have become flooring, millwork and beams for new homes and remodels. Willie travels the globe seeking out antique heart pine, oak, hickory, chestnut and other antique hardwoods found in barns, factories, mills and breweries, and he used some of his best finds to build his home in West Virginia. His own home, a hodgepodge of boards picked up from river bottoms and abandoned buildings, welcomes you like an old sweater.

Clad in weathered cypress board-and-batten siding, the home blends beautifully with its wooded site. Inside, Willie had kitchen counters built with reclaimed Russian oak from 1920s railroad cars and cabinets crafted from local wormy chestnut that's no longer available in North America because it was decimated by blight in the 1930s. Redwood porch flooring is from a Richmond, Virginia, water tank, and the porch's columns are from a 19th-century Massachusetts textile mill.

When Willie gives tours of his house, he regales visitors with each wood's history, with no small amount of awe that it has weathered so magnificently. His house is a temple, an ode to wood's longevity and magic. "I love the fact that every part you see is reclaimed wood," Willie says of his house. "Old timber has a warmth and a patina that cannot be duplicated."

You don't have to grow up in Morocco, circle your county gathering up building materials or own a salvaged-wood business to find great stuff to build with. As they've become more popular in recent years, salvaged materials have become easier to find — in salvage yards and resale stores, through classified ads and online.

The Internet is a good source for hard-to-find items, structural lumber and even some hardware — and has made it easier for everyone (not just those in rural areas where barns are falling down or urban areas where buildings are being dismantled) to use salvaged wood. When buying anything online, be aware that digital come-ons can be deceiving. Ideally, you would run your hands over wood to see if there's chemistry and study antique doors' quirks and quality before you commit. Online sources that allow you to search only in your area, such as craigslist, are a better bet, and local green building groups often have directories and chat groups. If you're lucky enough to have one within driving distance, a salvage yard is where the magic happens.

Spending an afternoon at Boulder's ReSource yard, checking out the stacks of lumber, doors, bricks and fencing, basins and radiators, is one of my favorite things to do. I could go home with anything: an old metal farm door to cover the wood fence behind my grill, a funky

artificial serenity

In tea, there is a saying: "To become rusty is all right; to make something rusty is no good." This will bring *sabasu*, the artificial serenity that comes when things are made to look shabby. Purposefully distressing anything in the tea room is considered gauche.

Guy and Kay Baker and their three sons built their home using salvaged materials from every town in Randolph County, Alabama.

hanging lamp for my bedroom (that I had to talk the manager out of, because it really did look great hanging in the yard's entry gate). With a little help from the broken mirror shards I picked up by the "free" swap pile, I found all the tile I needed to mosaic my townhouse's back patio for $10 at ReSource.

When I'm in the market for any home-improvement or repair part, I start at ReSource before I hit Home Depot. I've picked up unglamorous hoses and screens for half of what I would pay retail. So even if a $10 window frame for an art project captures my heart while I'm there, I'm still saving money — and keeping garbage out of the landfill. Last year ReSource diverted 2,500 tons of material — a small fraction of the 136 million tons of construction and demolition waste that the United States generates annually. But a start.

good wood

Salvaged flooring, recovered from old buildings and from logs lost at the bottom of rivers in the late 19th century, can cost almost double what new flooring costs — but you get higher-quality wood from trees up to 400 years old. And for every 2,000 square feet of flooring you use, you spare an acre of woodland.

This bathroom was built using scrap materials and junk yard finds.

safer salvage

Salvage yards are full of junk. Be prepared to dig through piles of crusty windows and rusty fixtures before you find what you're looking for. Salvage yards often — but not always — group items by category, but the user-friendliness ends there. Salvaging is dirty. Be on the lookout for rusty nails and tin, and make sure your tetanus shot is up to date. Always check for loose nails before grabbing hold of old wood, and be aware that the paint clinging to that wood might contain lead.

- If you suspect any item has lead paint, don't strip it yourself. Seal it with clear polyurethane to keep the distressed look, or paint over the old paint.

- Check all items carefully and be honest about whether it's too rotten to resurrect. Attempting to salvage the unsalvageable leads to frustration and wastes your time.

- Check shutters for loose corner joints and broken slats. A few of these may be acceptable if you don't need functional shutters, but too many will look dilapidated.

- Check stone items for cracks and stains; these are almost impossible to fix.

- When salvaging bricks, find out when they were fired. Bricks made before 1940, when production controls were tightened, aren't as durable..

doors

These doors reflect happy memories.

I found these funky French doors at Boulder's ReSource, a recycled building materials center. They were shorter than current code, so I had a carpenter refit the door jamb in my old house for them. When I lived in that house, I looked through the doors every day, at my kids playing in the back yard. I could look up from cooking and see the reflection of a swing moving or, later, a body bouncing on a trampoline. After I moved out, my ex-husband had the doors removed. I have them now in my small dining room. I can't afford a carpenter, and I don't have a doorway to fill, so I will paste old photographs and rice paper over the glass panes and hang the doors from the ceiling. They will be an ancestor altar.

wood wise: a guide to reclaimed planks

Red Oak: This strong, heavy wood with a straight grain and pinkish red heart was used as barn siding, planking and flooring.

White Oak: This durable, rot-resistant, yellowish wood was used in post-and-beam construction, factory roofs, barn siding and flooring.

Tulip Poplar: This yellowish, uniformly textured wood once used for log cabins is easy to work with.

Chestnut: This golden to reddish wood, once used in post-and-beam construction, planking, flooring and siding, is now rare and desirable.

Weathered old barn doors are now in demand.

Everybody needs beauty as well as bread, places to play in and pray in where nature may heal and cheer and give strength to the body and soul.

— John Muir

Ancestral photos and items with history give your home soul.

soul

Years ago I was the editor of a high-end design magazine featuring second and third homes, usually decorated by professionals. The homes were lovely, often exquisitely appointed with wabi-sabi-ish décor such as primitive wooden troughs and antique Mexican doors. And all too often, they were dead spaces. Nothing but showcases for the designers, the rooms were accommodating but offputting, luxurious but cold. I wasn't surprised that the homeowners spent barely two or three weeks a year there. Those houses, so pretty in pictures, were all too often about pretension and compromise, and you felt that when you walked in.

When I bought my first house in Boulder, Colorado, I wanted it to be the antithesis of these soulless places. I wanted everything in my family's home to be hand-picked and have a good story behind it. I would not bring in just anything because I'd gotten tired of shopping. That meant our young family used rickety hand-me-down kitchen table chairs as dining chairs until I found mid-century Knoll chairs that I loved (and could afford). Those sturdy chairs held up through toddlers and meals, parties and magazine staff meetings, and served as footstools and blanket-fort armature for more than a decade. They

Machine-made things are children of the brain; they are not very human. The more they spread, the less the human being is needed.

— Soetsu Yanagi

were hip and looked right in our 1955 ranch house. Piece by piece, over the next 13 years, our house came together like that.

I learned a lot in that house. Living without the lamp that would complete a corner or art for a big blank wall wasn't easy, but every time I made do with something because I was tired of waiting for the right thing to show up, I regretted it. For the rest of my days in that house, I cursed at and apologized for the ugly pink vinyl kitchen floor that my then husband and I compromised on at the end of an over-budget remodel. The floor responded insultingly by developing a big seam between the plastic sheets. That gap grew wider year by year, reminding me daily that I chose expediency over soul.

Nearly everything in our homes is made by machines, which is perhaps why we're so touched by goods that remember the hands and the heart that made them. Many Eastern religions, Shintoism in

My former husband and I slept for years under a duvet cover made from two sheets stitched together, until we could afford this handmade quilt. We spent an afternoon sifting through calicos and flannels in a quilt shop on the shores of Minnesota's Lake Superior, pulling together just the right combination of sage greens, midnight blues and rusty reds. Over the next couple of months, into the winter, the local women created our quilt during their weekly bee. I love this quilt, but it's reserved for my guests since I've divorced. I'm sure the women of Grand Marais understand.

Hand-stitched by a quilting circle in Minnesota, this quilt also holds memories.

particular, believe that everything — from the human being to the speck of dust — carries a vibration. A piece made slowly and lovingly by hand, rather than by a jarring and impersonal machine, holds the steady, solid vibrations of its maker. "The making of ceramics and our attitude toward living are closely related," potter Shiho Kanzaki says. "An attitude of disarray toward living can cause us to make works that have a 'wrong spirit' or are without soul." Imagine the spirit that lives in plastic gadgets made by soulless machines run by sleep-deprived wage slaves in the Philippines.

Surrounding myself with things that real people made invites a tiny piece of each craftsman into my space, subtly changing the energy. I bring honor into my house when I serve potatoes in the purple bowl thrown by a potter from my hometown in Iowa or place flowers in the balloon-shaped water jug made by a man I met in Asheville, North Carolina, fired in a kiln powered by methane gas from a landfill. When I brew tea in my mustard yellow pot, I remember one of the best days I spent in Japan. I'm drawn to all of these things for their beauty and utility, but it's the people who made them — and the stories behind them — that make the difference.

American sculptor Kiki Smith says pottery's magic is its utility. "The owner acts with it in a direct way: own it, use it," she says. "In that way it is like jewelry. One doesn't simply stand back and observe and admire as one is likely to do with a painting or sculpture." Touching and interacting with fine, heavy pottery and hand-stitched textiles gives me something to appreciate every day. My sister Stefanie's hand-stitched quilts keep my kids warm at night and remind them of family in Iowa who love them. When we watch TV, we wrap up in afghans so finely crocheted (by my grandmothers and a friend) that they've stood up to being TV room blankets in a house full of kids for 16 years. The sea-green water jug from North Carolina takes center stage on the credenza in my little townhouse. Its narrow neck forces me to be sparing with the branches or flowers I choose for it that week. (It would never accommodate a cellophane-wrapped "garden bouquet.") It looks great with three early pussy willows or one bare winter branch, which saves me a bundle on grocery store flowers and keeps me in touch with how the seasons are changing right outside my door.

My father built this table from a beautiful slab of maple.

make yourself at home

Take a look around your house. Can you tell a story about most of the objects you see? Does your home say anything about you? If your world seems a little cold, start injecting yourself into your home environment in small ways.

1. Replace canned art with a framed child's painting or a photo from your last vacation.
2. Build shelves and surround yourself with the books you love. (Books are a dying wabi-sabi artifact whose full loss is yet to be felt.)
3. Make a rag rug (or have it made) out of clothes your kids have outgrown.

Family photos warm up a dining area.

*I abhor a room
that demands such
perfection that the
only thing out of
place in it is you.*

— Mark Hampton

CHAPTER 13

imperfection

Perfect Minimalist rooms are beautiful (even admirable) but offputting. The right vase placed in just the right spot injects the optimal color pop. Everything unnecessary has been eliminated so that light, clean lines and fine finishes can carry the room. Fringe and family photos are verboten. Well-behaved pets that don't shed might be allowed (if they look good curled up just so on the ottoman).

Architect John Pawson (dubbed "the man who made Martha Stewart rethink chintz" by *Time* magazine) says Minimalist interiors offer a liberation that's not possible "if one is distracted by the trivial." But Pawson is distracted by his clients' inability to stop messing with his austere interiors. "There's no stopping them," he says. "There's always something lying around that alters the focus of the whole room." Like Frank Lloyd Wright, whose response to clients' uncouth tastes was to build in all the furnishings, Pawson designed a collection of sanctioned objects for the clutter-prone that includes a bronze bowl, a white lacquer and cedar tray, and a wooden cylinder candle holder.

The problem with perfect Minimalist rooms is that they don't work for real people, who are messy sometimes and need places to store stuff. They look great in photographs and work well in theory, but most people don't want to live in a place where leaving a coffee cup on the side table is a problem. Even Minimalism's champions agree that it can make for a stressful household. "Minimalism requires a discipline that most people don't have," admits architect Deborah Berke (dubbed "Miss Minimalism" by *Wallpaper*). "And it makes anyone who can't resist buying things or doesn't put stuff away or control their children feel lousy about themselves." Brian Carter, the University of Michigan's architecture chair who champions British Minimalism, confessed to the *Minneapolis Star-Tribune*, "I hate to sound like my mother, but it is nerve-racking to imagine trying to vacuum those white walls without scuffing them."

"If minimalism looks like it's hard work, that's often because it is," designer Terence Conran writes in *Easy Living*. Conran's more relaxed style of Minimalism allows for some imperfection, a personal touch or two and a whisper of whimsy while still providing "the play of natural light, the sheer dynamic of space, and the subtleties of form and texture" that Minimalism does so well. Architect Tadao Ando, influenced by the simple, rustic farmhouses of his native Japan, uses humble materials to carve out spaces that reduce architecture "to the extremes of simplicity and an aesthetic so devoid of actuality and

perfectly imperfect

When Sen no Rikyu was learning tea ceremony under Jo-o, his master asked him to tend to his garden. Rikyu cleaned up debris and raked the paths until it was perfect, then scrutinized the immaculate grounds. Before presenting his work, he shook a cherry tree, causing a few blossoms to spill randomly onto the ground.

attributes that it approaches theories of ma, or nothingness." In his wabi-sabi approach to Minimalism (which he criticizes as "completely ignoring all human considerations"), Ando predicts that Modernism and Humanism can coexist, "even if, during our century, they have more often been in conflict."

Super-lush interior design magazines make me neurotic. I'm drawn to them like an addict for a fix — into lush, seductive page after page of stylish, expensive, perfect rooms that I could never in a million years afford. Everything, down to the Andy Goldsworthy books on the tufted ottoman, is considered and carefully placed. Anything jarring or unintended has been Photoshopped out. The photos are delicious printed perfection. I crave those sleek, dry-martini living rooms and plush, draperied boudoirs, stripped of all life — no toaster ovens or clock radios, melted and forgotten candles, dog food bowls or granny-square afghans crocheted by grandma.

Today, thank goodness, we are more concerned with the personal than with perfection.

— Billy Baldwin

Because I'm in the business, I know what it takes to produce those magazine hero shots. It takes a crew. We move out daily life's detritus — receipt piles, paperback novels and prescription bottles — and we pull in sake sets, placing them just so. Rearrange furniture, fix lighting, plump pillows, fix lighting again. We pore over the computer screen, checking for the tiniest flaws, wilted petals or wayward fringe. We rearrange the folds of the draperies. We change out the tall vase for the short one and check the screen again.

No one lives like this. Real people leave mail piles in the entry and let the flowers go a little too long (if they have them at all). Real people roller-skate in the house and let the dog on the bed. They have unpredictable cats. They leave scars.

My sister Stacey used to remodel high-end homes in Santa Monica. She spent thousands of clients' dollars on Viking stoves and granite countertops, designer paint and custom cabinetry for fresh, new living spaces. During the final walk-through, inevitably, the clients would pick out every nick in the woodwork, the smallest scratch in the floor. It didn't matter that the house would be covered with little dings within six months of their moving back in. The clients wanted their house to be *perfect*. "We would go back a few months later to take photographs, and sure enough, the baseboards would be all smudged and the refrigerator full of fingerprints," she says. "And what would you expect? These people *live* there."

Without people, and their traces, a home is just a house. We shot a house in Berkeley, California, many years ago that had been staged to attract a heftier sale price. It was lovely, with tasteful furnishings and objects as perfectly bland as the classical music that played all day on a continual loop. We hardly had to do a thing to prepare each room to be shot; the stager had even left open books with reading glasses and breakfast trays on beds. The home photographed well enough, but the sparkle of the woman who remodeled it was lost. Her favorite blankets and her quirky artwork didn't stand a chance in all that commodified perfection. Her home had become real estate.

I lived for 13 years in a most imperfect home in Boulder, and I loved to complain. The ugly metal picture window in the living room was inefficient and made the house look dated. The bathrooms were tiny and poorly designed. The kitchen layout didn't work. The yard had a mind of its own. I would get so caught up in all my chatter about what was wrong that I would forget how thrilled we'd been to score that house, flanked by two wise maples that provided welcome shade in summer and strong arms for swings and tree houses. I couldn't see the dramatic mountain views or appreciate the woodstove's cozy winter warmth when I was complaining about the god-awful kitchen floor.

The home I live in now is far from perfect. It's small, and I don't really love the finishes. It has no curb appeal. Those flaws are easy to

Everything has its wonders, even darkness and silence, and I learn, whatever state I may be in, therein to be content.

— Helen Keller

the candle trick

It's hard to relax at the end of a long day when the sofa is covered in dog hair and the breakfast bowls are caked with dried oatmeal and the mail basket in the entry hall is overflowing.

Try this very simple solution. Throw the dishes in the sink to soak and throw a blanket over the sofa. Turn out all the lights. Take a match to two or three candles, placed strategically away from the dirty dishes and the dog hair so that their light pools only on empty space. Relax. Nothing looks bad in candlelight.

Treat yourself to candlelight.

overlook, though, when sun streams through the kitchen skylight or I'm enjoying the magnificent views from my back deck. As a single mother on a limited budget, I didn't think I'd find a comfortable place to shelter myself and my kids in the city that I love (which is, unfortunately, expensive). I'm so grateful for this place that I can't see its flaws.

Dwelling on our home's negative aspects will never bring peace. Remembering what's great about where we live — friends in the neighborhood, a nearby park, affordability — just might. If you need help remembering why your home rocks, put a list of its attributes on your refrigerator. Read it the next time you curse the inadequate lighting in the entryway or the leaky single-pane windows on a frosty morning. Even if the only thing on your list is that you have a home, you can consider yourself blessed.

peace cracks

On my desk I keep a mug with this saying: "Peace. It does not mean to be in a place where there is no noise, trouble or hard work. It means to be in the midst of those things and still be calm in your heart." The first time I poured coffee into the mug, it seeped out through a hairline crack in the bottom and spilled all over the countertop. Now I use it to hold pens and pencils and remind myself that my life is riddled with imperfections. The imperfections are funny, and my attempts at perfection are even funnier.

*The lust for comfort,
that stealthy thing
that enters the house
a guest, and then
becomes a host, and
then, a master.*

— Kahlil Gibran

CHAPTER 14

hospitality

Decades ago, as the young wife of a New York advertising executive, I decorated the living area of our Tribeca loft with sculptural, hip furniture made by famous designers. The lollipop chairs and corkscrew sofa looked great on the mosaic marble floor that our friend Carlos had created for us, but I made a young decorator's common mistake: I created a living space without any comfortable places to sit or lie down. People would go into the living room to look at the artwork and admire the floor (which really was spectacular), then come back to the unfinished kitchen to hang out. Once some friends of my parents spent the night in our guest loft, and the husband had insomnia. When his wife urged him to go sit in the living room so she could get some sleep, he hissed, "There's nowhere to *sit* in there." That story became legend in my family.

My inhospitable living room-cum-museum taught me the importance of comfort — an attribute that increasingly trumps fashion in everything from my shoes to my sofa as I grow older. I no longer stay in chic modernist hotel rooms with cold concrete floors, harsh lighting and flimsy bedspreads just because they're hip and on the right side of town. I don't stay in hotels where the windows don't open. Every room in my townhouse (except the kitchen) has a soft seat and a blanket to curl up with, gentle lighting and a deep, delicious rug. Every room invites people to stay — and they do, curled up in afghans and sipping tea.

In the decades since that first attempt at interior design, the most important lesson I've learned is that, no matter how hip or elegant, a room doesn't work if no one uses it. And no one uses it if it isn't comfortable. *House Beautiful* editor Elizabeth Gordon reminded readers of this again and again as what she called the "cult of austerity" took hold in American design. "Good modern design offers comfort *and* performance *and* beauty," she wrote.

I wanted to give my kids the elaborate Christmas Eve memories that my mom had given my siblings and me. When I was growing up, we invited friends and neighbors for an open house, and I remember it as a magical night. The dining table groaned with hors d'oeuvres, wine flowed freely, Christmas carols played on the reel-to-reel and a fire crackled in the fireplace. It was Currier and Ives perfect, and I had no idea what it took to make that happen. My mom had my two older

After all, what is your hosts' purpose in having a party? Surely not for you to enjoy yourself; if that were their sole purpose, they'd have simply sent champagne and women over to your place by taxi.

— P. J. O'Rourke

comforts

Simple steps to make your home more welcoming.

- Turn off harsh overhead lights and use table lamps or candles.
- Cover sofa pillows in a gingham that fades.
- Have extra blankets.
- Make sure there's a place to rest a book and a cup by every chair in your house.
- Sleep in your own guest room and see if you've provided everything your guests need.
- Replace inoperable windows with double-hungs or casements that open wide.

zelda's chair

I bought this chair in Soho just before I left New York. I fell in love with its cold green iron and its clean Deco lines, muscular but curvy. The gallery owner told me it was made in the 1920s for a sanitarium in upstate New York, and I imagined Zelda Fitzgerald (or one of her friends) lounging on the lawn, looking out over the river below. I had the chair shipped to my new place in Chicago, and for a while it was the only piece of furniture I owned.

It's not a great chair to have if you have only one chair to offer. Cold iron against the back of your head and bars pushing up against your knees are probably reason enough not to land yourself in a sanitarium. I had to dress my chair. With a sheepskin and several deep pillows, this chair became a cozy nest. Now it's my favorite place to curl up with a book or just sit and look out the window.

Beautiful…but uncomfortable.

sisters to watch my brother and me, and she worked part-time. I'm not saying she wasn't amazing, but she had some resources I didn't have.

When my kids were very young, I invited all my friends and neighbors for an annual Christmas Eve gathering. The party sent me into overdrive. Deep into the long, long winter nights leading up to that party, I made appetizers, wrapped gifts for Santa to distribute to all the kids, cleaned my Christmas china and baked cookies. By Christmas Eve day, I was exhausted, and my kids were tired of being ignored.

One year, as I frantically searched for coconut while swiping at the filthy baseboards that I hadn't noticed before and arranging evergreen boughs for the table, my three-year-old daughter, Cree, kept asking me to play. I kept saying no, and she kept asking. I snapped. "Can't you see how much I have to do?" I yelled. "I haven't even set the table yet. *And don't crack those nuts in here!*"

Cree burst into tears. "Mommy, I hate the Christmas Eve party!" she said. "I hate Christmas Eve!"

She got my attention. I sat down on the floor, leaned against the dirty baseboard, and took Cree into my lap so we could crack nuts and throw the shells on the floor. As the afternoon light dimmed, we

humble invitation

In an attempt to outshine Japan's most famous tea master, Sen no Rikyu, Emperor Toyotoma Hideyoshi covered his tea house with gold leaf. It didn't work. An invitation to Rikyu's simple, rustic, thatched tea hut remained much more coveted. Some claim that Hideyoshi's anger over this public injustice contributed to his demand that Rikyu perform ritual suicide (but that's debatable).

toriawase: play with the seasons

Tea ceremony deeply honors every season as it passes, injecting subtle symbolic messages known as *toriawase* throughout. During a tea ceremony in Tokyo in early June, I was served a beautiful sky blue sweet (*omogashi*) with four sections, evoking (but not mimicking) the hydrangeas blooming outside. A single peony, wrapped in a tight ball, graced the alcove reserved for a seasonal Zen scroll and flowers (*tokonoma*). Tea was served in a wide, shallow bowl, in accordance with Rikyu's rule: "In the summer try to bring out the feeling of coolness, in the winter the feeling of warmth." Steamed sweets and tall, narrow bowls that let vapor wash over and warm our faces would have been winter fare.

Bach Train

simple hospitality

Your guest is your first, your last, and your everything.

1. Serve a variety of food so that everyone's diet (from vegan to Atkins) is covered.
2. If it's cold outside, greet them with a hot drink and invite them in to a room warmed by a roaring fire. If it's warm, play tropical music and pass out fans.
3. Keep their drinks filled (unless they are tipsy).
4. Watch for wallflowers, and spend as much time as you can with them.
5. Introduce guests to one another and stick around to spark conversations.

Photo courtesy of chocolatereview.co.uk

Finish off your hospitality with small finishing touches such as a chocolate stir stick for warm milk.

lit candles and saw that by their flickering light no one could see our baseboards. No one missed the coconut in the appetizers, either.

That was the best Christmas Eve party we ever had — and the last. No one trusted me not turn back into the hostess from hell, and I didn't miss the frenzy. I'd always been too busy refreshing appetizer trays and drinks to enjoy Christmas Eve, and I wasn't creating the magical memories for my kids that I'd hoped for. When we stopped having our bash, our neighbors Dan and Marcia started having a quieter and saner Christmas Day open house where everyone could share their leftovers from the night before. Dan and Marcia's party became a comfortable tradition because they didn't feel compelled to show off their culinary skills or impress people with their spotless home. Their party had the casual camaraderie of an impromptu popcorn party in a college dorm room.

You can't be a good hostess when you're fried and frenzied. If you don't have the time and energy to pull off a big bash without a meltdown, keep entertaining casual. Invite guests for hot chocolate and cookies or lemon cake and sorbet in the back yard. Without all the fuss, you can focus on paying attention to the reason you threw the party: your guests (despite what P. J. O'Rourke might think).

wabi wealth

As the most revered tastemaker of his time, Sen no Rikyu made a fine living selling the rustic pottery and bamboo vases that he used in his tea ceremony. In perhaps the longest-running celebrity-endorsed merchandise line, Rikyu collaborated with a tile-maker named Chojiro to make Raku-style tea bowls that are coveted by tea ceremony aficionados today.

Chris Greene

There's only two things that money can't buy, and that's true love and homegrown tomatoes.

— Guy Clark

CHAPTER 15

Ssimplicity

MY FIRST WABI-SABI CONFESSION: I HAVE FAVORITE TV SHOWS. I live in a townhouse with four people and three TVs (flat screens, two of them in bedrooms), which keeps down arguments over what to watch (or play) but isn't at all wabi-sabi. I'm a little embarrassed that my family's succumbed to TV culture, but I'm not ready to kill my televisions. Sometimes I like zoning out with caramel corn, watching *American Pickers*. I'm a wabi-fraudie.

I have other confessions. Not too many years ago, I shopped so much at Nordstrom that I had a favorite shoe salesperson (who taught me that "spending" and "saving" — like during their semi-annual sale — is called "spaving"). I've spent ridiculous amounts on curtains and used the word "need" in association with luxuries. I'm pretty sure I'm too sexy for my seven-year-old Honda Civic Hybrid. I'm a materialist.

I've bought the hype. It makes me cringe, but my desire for the latest, fastest model wins out over thoughtful frugality more than I want it to. I've downsized considerably since I divorced, but I still think I need the most Gs for my smart phone. Even my kids understand that every technological advancement is another way to get them to buy more stuff — and they always want the stuff. They hang out in a mall (or "retail resort," as the developers called the shopping center down the road from us when it was built), and they know more brand logos than Colorado native plants. (If I have to be honest, I do, too.)

Shopping is entertainment, and shopping is therapy. "The ugly side of consumerism exists because there is something deeply meaningful about shopping," sociologist Dan Cook told *The Christian Science Monitor* in 2002. "Shopping is the provisioning of care, and the marketplace brings social intercourse and cultural interchange." Slow Design founder Alastair Fuad-Luke writes that consumerism has replaced religious ritual in modern culture. "Shopping is the new religion, the shopping centres and malls the cathedrals to which the populace flock," he writes. "Consumerism has usurped thousands of years of symbolic ritualism of nature's seasons, religion, monarchy and patriarchy."

When my marriage was crumbling, I shopped so much online that I knew my credit card number by heart. (That came in handy a couple times when I forgot my wallet.) I shopped to stuff the deep hole I

natural order

Two hundred years ago, Japanese Zen monk and renowned calligrapher Sengai produced a scroll that sent a wealthy patron into a rage. "A parent dies, a child dies, then a grandchild dies," the artist had written. When the warlord complained furiously about the obvious, even elementary, message, Sengai gently rebuffed him.

"There can be no greater happiness," he said, "than to live a life that follows the natural order of things."

felt inside, and I ended up with a closet full of really nice clothes and accessories that I've been selling off at the consignment store since I got divorced. I like to think that I've become less of a materialist, but the truth is I've just changed my focus. Now I'm a secondhand materialist.

On Saturday mornings I get my daughter Cree out of the mall and on a tour of our area's best clothing consignment shops (where I do try to sell two things for every one I buy). Cree loves secondhand shopping as much as I do because the hunting is unpredictable and takes a good eye. It's more challenging than the bland, "this season's look" retail resort experience, and both of us have an equal chance of finding something satisfying (despite our very different taste). One day I found a leather coat with fake fur trim that reminds me of Kate Hudson in "Almost Famous." It's my favorite coat. Cree thinks it looks ratty and asks me not to wear it.

Thorstein Veblen coined the term "conspicuous consumption," for people's proclivity to buy things that proved how wealthy they were, in 1899. As members of each social group strive to obtain what the class above them is buying, Veblen argued, luxury standards are pushed higher and higher. A hundred years later, accelerated by globalization, this striving for a little too much house, granite counter-tops and Burberry plaid has hit a ceiling. The sub-prime mortgage crisis and investment bank failures of 2008 ripped the bottom out of the Disney-drenched, credit-fueled simulacrum.

In October 2008, as panicked consumers watched their 401ks dry up — but before the full extent of the protracted recession had hit — historian Steven Fraser declared in *The New York Times* that we'd reached "the end of the era of conspicuous displays of wealth." Wall Street fat cats and ostentatious CEOs would continue to indulge in $30 million houses and $6,000 shower curtains — accoutrements of our modern gilded age. But when the economy crashed, making decent middle-class wages scarce for everyone — not just the unskilled

To found a great empire for the sole purpose of raising up a people of customers may at first sight appear a project fit only for a nation of shopkeepers.

— Adam Smith,
  The Wealth of Nations

be a non-consumer

- Start seeing yourself in your intentions, your actions and your relationships — not in what you buy.
- Eliminate one half-hour of shopping (whether at the mall, online or through catalogs) each week and spend it instead with a child or an elderly person.

- Spend as much time and attention maintaining and repairing your household goods as you do buying new ones.
- Share a lawn mower or a power drill with the neighbors.
- Slipcover.

workers who had been struggling against de-industrialization and outsourcing for decades — the simulacrum tipped. It became uncool to flaunt your bonus.

Even those of us who don't get Wall Street bonuses have been sobered. For the first time in decades, we're saving more than we're spending. We've stopped buying things we can't afford and started putting money in savings. In 2010, for the first time since the early 1980s, housing size dropped. "We continue to move away from the 'McMansion' chapter of residential design, with more demand for practicality throughout the home," American Institute of Architects chief economist Kermit Baker reported. "And with that there has been a drop off in the popularity of upscale property enhancements such as formal landscaping, decorative water features, tennis courts and gazebos." We don't want to emulate *Lifestyles of the Rich and Famous* so much anymore. We're morphing.

In 2010, Wanda Urbanska, star of the PBS show *Simple Living with Wanda Urbanska* and the author of eight books on the subject, told *Natural Home* that the economic downturn had "pushed us to a better place — a slower, thriftier place." Wanda said that no one was asking anymore whether simple living was a good idea. "Everyone wants to know how to get started," she said. As the simulacrum sinks, simplicity is becoming the ultimate luxury.

Letting go of commitments we're not fully committed to and stuff we don't care about (but have to take care of) is a gift greater than gold — and an ability worth cultivating.

My first taste of simplicity's promise came from Duane Elgin's 1981 bestseller, *Voluntary Simplicity*. Elgin showed me that putting less energy into systems I'd like to see transmogrify gives me more time to focus on what I love. His brand of simple living — consciously chosen, deliberate and intentional — is about paring down possessions to free up time and energy for what really matters. Less stuff means more

I want to spend the time I have doing things that make my heart rage.

— Buck Howard

living the life

My kids and I visited Denise Franklin's solidly built 280-square-foot pine cottage in Oliver, British Columbia, in late summer, when wildfires were raging across the Okanagan mountains. Aptly named Quietude, Denise's home provides "a place to pray, meditate, prepare my food and entertain my friends, and a warm place to lay my head at night." We felt the magic.

Quietude is tiny, but it's well designed and it works. Cree fell in love with its compact coziness and especially envied the sleeping loft. Stacey asked many questions as Denise showed us her productive vegetable gardens and root cellar shelves lined with preserved fruits and vegetables for the coming winter. As evening fell, we all sat comfortably around Denise's dining table and swapped stories with her and architect Henry Yorke Mann as she prepared salmon with fresh-picked carrots and squash for dinner. A cool breeze blew through from the front door to the back, and distant wildfire smoke made for a brilliant sunset as we finished our rhubarb cake. That night, the kids and I slept like logs in a tiny bunk house (not even big enough for all our luggage), looking forward to Denise's special oatmeal with preserved home-grown fruit in the morning.

To a couple of suburban kids who spend most of their time texting, video gaming and Facebooking (and their mom, who's guilty of a couple of those and more), Denise's deeply simple lifestyle was a revelation. She lives the good life that some of us get to experience and many of us hold onto as a "someday." She grows good food that she eats and shares. She has just enough house to handle, and no mortgage (because she built it for $28,000). She skis, takes walks with her dog and makes stained glass. She has no TV — something my kids didn't even seem to notice.

In Quietude, Denise has created a place that encourages kindness, contentment and sharing — anything else is superfluous. "I've been in here 11 years, and I feel more thankful every day," she says. "I still don't want any more space. I just don't *need*."

My kids and I brought too much luggage.

Denise Franklin lives simply and seasonally.

time to spend with family, friends or nature — a philosophy simple enough for even the most complicated people (like me). Still, the concept was academic until my divorce forced me to move from a house to a townhouse. Now I understand the benefits.

Living in a small space keeps me from acquiring things. I've furnished my entire townhouse without ever getting out the credit card. I like sharing amenities, such as the swimming pool, and responsibilities, such as garbage collection, and I like running into neighbors when I walk my dog, Rug. I can walk Rug through pretty, shaded paths within our cluster of townhouses or along a ridge outside my back door, overlooking a valley with a working farm. (At night we hear coyotes.) My tiny back garden is just big enough to grow a couple of culinary and medicinal plants and enclose a cozy outdoor conversation spot. I like not battling knotweed or trying to grow grass. Except for storage, my little house has just enough of everything.

Sometimes I like to sit a while on my back deck, looking out at the wild grasses and the big, open sky, watching the cows graze in the fields beyond. A half hour will go by, the moon will come up, and I'll just sit. I'll watch the hawks circle and the ravens scold, and sometimes in late fall pairs of geese fly by, alarmingly low. I sit, an accidental *wabibito*, enjoying my life's gifts.

Every day around sunset, the man who lives at the end of our row shows up in our back window. He stands in the same spot, perfectly framed by our sliding glass doors, wearing khakis and a button-down shirt. In winter he wears a light jacket. For a half hour or so (I've never timed him), he leans against the wooden rail fence at the top of the ridge and looks out. When one of us spots him, we mark the in-between moment: time to turn off the computer and put away homework. The man in our view reminds us to stop for a minute and just look. Then it's time to think about dinner.

My hat has come apart during a long journey. I am a wabi man who has tried and known every wabi thing.

— Matsuo Basho,
The Winter Days

Matej Franó

wabi-sabi in the real world

Some day — maybe even some day soon — you'll start scouring salvage yards and flea markets for wabi-sabi furnishings. Some day — maybe even some day soon — you'll clear all the clutter out of your living space. In the meantime, you'd like to start bringing wabi-sabi into your home and into your life right now. You can start by taking these simple, basic steps. You'll be amazed at the difference they can make.

- One day a week, wash the dinner dishes by hand. Taking on this task alone allows you quiet, uninterrupted time to think — or not think.
- Pay attention to your daily bread. Is the food you're eating in season, and is it available locally? Through the meals you choose and prepare, you can connect with the earth's cycles and with the place where you live — and live a healthier life. Buy food from your local farmers' markets and ask the produce manager at your grocery store where different items came from.
- Next time you sweep the floor, consider it a meditation. Opt for the broom over the Dirt Devil.
- When you're invited to someone's house or even just to a meeting, bring a small gift — nothing extravagant, just a small gesture (a jar of home-made jam, apples from your tree or a luxurious bar of soap) that lets them know they're appreciated.
- Offer everyone who comes to visit a cup of tea. Serve it in pretty cups with a little something sweet. If no one comes by, enjoy a cup of tea by yourself in the late afternoon.
- Keep one vase in your home filled with seasonal flowers.

- Take a walk every day. Let this be your opportunity to open up your senses and to experience the changing seasons.

- Learn to knit or crochet.

- Next time you buy something, stop and ask questions. Who made it? How was it made? Where does it come from?

resources

CHAPTER 1: Chasing Wabi-Sabi

The Good Life Center at Forest Farm
Harborside, Maine
goodlife.org

Shiho Kanzaki
Koka Shiga, Japan
the-anagama.com

CHAPTER 2:
Teasing Out Its Roots:
Zen, Tea and Wabi-Sabi

The Urasenke Foundation
urasenke.org
instruction and information about the
Way of Tea

CHAPTER 3:
Feeling Its Influence:
Wabi-Sabi Through Time

William Morris Society
of the United States
Washington, D.C.
morrissociety.org

William Morris Society of Canada
Toronto, Ontario
wmsc.ca

George Nakashima Woodworker
New Hope, Pennsylvania
nakashimawoodworker.com

The Nakashima Foundation for Peace
New Hope, Pennsylvania
nakashimafoundation.org

Eames Office
Santa Monica, California
eamesoffice.com

Thos. Moser Cabinetmakers
Auburn, Maine
thosmoser.com

Slow Design
slowdesign.org

Free Tea Party
freeteaparty.org

CHAPTER 4: Slow

Project Laundry List
laundrylist.org

CHAPTER 6: Craft

American Craft Council
craftcouncil.org

American Needlepoint Guild
needlepoint.org

American Quilters Society
americanquilter.com

National Basketry Organization
nationalbasketry.org

National Quilting Association
nqaquilts.org

Textile Society of America
textilesociety.org

World Crafts Council
worldcraftscouncil.org

Interweave Press
Loveland, Colorado
interweave.com

ReadyMade magazine
readymade.com

RePlayGround
replayground.com

Craft Schools

**Arrowmont School of Arts
and Crafts**
Gatlinburg, Tennessee
arrowmont.org

Penland School of Craft
penland.org

Pottery Northwest
Seattle, Washington
potterynorthwest.org

Baltimore Clayworks
Baltimore, Maryland
baltimoreclayworks.org

Brookfield Craft Center
Brookfield, Connecticut
brookfieldcraftcenter.org

Women's Studio Workshop
Rosendale, New York
wsworkshop.org

Worcester Center for Crafts
Worcester, Massachusetts
worcestercraftcenter.org

Haliburton School of the Arts
Haliburton, Ontario
haliburtonschoolofthearts.ca

Haystack Mountain School of Crafts
Deer Isle, Maine
haystack-mtn.org

John C. Campbell Folk School
Brasstown, North Carolina
folkschool.com

Mendocino Arts Center
Mendocino, California
mendocinoartcenter.org

Peters Valley Craft Center
Layton, New Jersey
pvcrafts.org

Museums

Mingei International Museum
San Diego, California
mingei.org

Museum of International Folk Art
Santa Fe, New Mexico
internationalfolkart.org/

Nippon Mingeikan
Japan Folk Craft Museum
Tokyo, Japan
mingeikan.or.jp/english/

Artists

Alabama Chanin Studio
Florence, Alabama
alabamachanin.com

Carlos Alves
Miami, Florida
carlosalvesmosaics.com

Jill Nokes
Austin, Texas
nokeslandscapedesign.com

Chapter 7: Cleanliness

Natural Home's **Guide to DIY Cleaners**
naturalhomemagazine.com/best
-green-cleaning-products-natural
-cleaners-nontoxic-cleaning.asp

Chapter 9: Space

Clutterless Recovery Groups
clutterless.org

National Association of Professional Organizers
Norcross, Georgia
napo.net

Unclutterer
unclutterer.com

Be Clutter Free
beclutter-free.com

Goodwill Industries International
Bethesda, Maryland
goodwill.org

craigslist
craigslist.com

NeighborGoods
neighborgoods.com

Chapter 10: Silence

Noise Free America
Albany, New York
noisefree.org

The Noise Pollution Clearinghouse
Montpelier Vermont
nonoise.org

World Forum for Acoustic Ecology
wfae.proscenia.net

Eco-Friendly Flooring
ecofriendlyflooring.com

Chapter 11: Sabi

Building Materials

Habitat for Humanity ReStores
habitat.org/env/restore.html

Building Materials Reuse Association
Beaverton, Oregon
bmra.org

Salvage Web
salvageweb.com

Historic House Parts
historichouseparts.com

Liz's Antique Hardware
Los Angeles, California
lahardware.com

Nor'East Architectural Antiques
South Hampton, New Hampshire
noreast1.com

Salvaged Wood and Flooring

Barnstormers Woodwork
Rhinebeck, New York
safesolutionsllc.com

Black's Farmwood
San Rafael, California
blacksfarmwood.com
reclaimed wood beams, flooring, siding

Carlisle Wide Plank Floors
wideplankflooring.com
reclaimed wood flooring

Conklin's Authentic Barnwood
conklinsbarnwood.com
antique barn wood and hand-hewn
beams

Duluth Timber
duluthtimber.com

Eco Timber
Denver, Colorado
ecotimber.com

Goodwin Heart Pine
heartpine.com
reclaimed wood flooring, millwork,
stair parts

Heartwood Pine
heartwoodpine.com

Mountain Lumber
Ruckersville, Virginia
mountainlumber.com

Antique and Thrift Shopping

Architectural Artifacts
architecturalartifacts.com
antique furniture

Kovels Online
kovels.com

The National Antique & Art Dealers
Association of America
naada.org

The Art & Antiques Dealers League
of America
aadla.com

Cleveland Art
Los Angeles, California
clevelandart.com

The Thrift Shopper
thethriftshopper.com

Flea USA
fleausa.com

Collecting and Home Furnishing
Directory
collectics.com

Garage Sales Tracker
garagesalestracker.com

Vintage Renewal
vintagerenewal.com

Antique Roadshow Online
pbs.org/wgbh/roadshow

CHAPTER 12: Soul

EnergyXChange Craft Incubator
Burnsville, North Carolina
energyxchange.org/craft/craftstudios

Aid to Artisans
West Hartford, Connecticut
aidtoartisans.org

American Art Pottery Association
aapa.info

Antiki Trading Company
antiki.com

Chista
New York, New York
chista.net

Craft Alliance
craftalliance.org

Etsy
etsy.com

Global Sistergoods
globalsistergoods.com

Manos de Madres
manosdemadres.org

Novica.com
novica.com

Serrv International
serrv.org

Ten Thousand Villages
tenthousandvillages.com

World of Good
worldofgood.com

Artful Home
artfulhome.com

Remodelista: Sourcebook for
the Considered Home
remodelista.com

CHAPTER 15: Simplicity

Awakening Earth
awakeningearth.org

Alternatives for Simple Living
simpleliving.org

Center for a New American Dream
newdream.org

Postconsumers
postconsumers.com

The Simplicity Forum
simplicityforum.org

The Simple Living Network
simpleliving.net

Simple Living with Wanda Urbanska
simplelivingtv.net

Take Back Your Time
timeday.org

Finishes and Furnishings, Flooring

APCOR Portuguese Cork Association
realcork.org
cork flooring

Armstrong World Industries
armstrong.com
recycled cork linoleum

Earth Weave Carpet Mills
Dalton, Georgia
earthweave.com
hemp and wool carpet

Eco-Friendly Flooring
Madison, Wisconsin
ecofriendlyflooring.com
cork, recycled glass tile, stone,
reclaimed wood

Fibreworks
fibreworks.com
natural fiber floor coverings

Forbo
forboflooringna.com
natural linoleum

US Floors
naturalcork.com
cork flooring

WE Cork
wecork.com
cork flooring

Wicanders Cork Flooring
wicanders.com
cork flooring

Paints, Plasters and Finishes

Agalia Natural Paints
aglaiapaint.com

American Clay
americanclay.com
clay plaster

AFM Safecoat
afmsafecoat.com
nontoxic paints and finishes

Anna Sova Luxury Organics
annasova.com
natural paint, texture, stucco

Auro
aurousa.com
natural paint

BioLime
biolime.com
natural stuccos, plasters and paint

Bioshield
bioshieldpaint.com
clay paints and plasters, natural
pigments

The Natural Finish
thenaturalfinish.com
natural oils, stains, paints, waxes

**The Old Fashioned Milk Paint
Company**
milkpaint.com

EcoHaus
ecohaus.com
environmental building supplies,
natural earth plaster

Vital Systems
vitalsystems.net
earthen and lime plasters

Rugs

Garuda Woven Art
garudawovenart.com
naturally dyed rugs

The Natural Carpet Company
naturalcarpetcompany.com
handwoven area rugs

Nizhoni Ranch Gallery
navajorug.com
Navajo rugs, sheep's wool rugs, wall
hangings

Prestige Mills
prestigemills.com
sisal carpet and rugs

Woven Legends
Philadelphia, Pennsylvania
wovenlegends.com
naturally dyed, handmade carpets
from handspun wool

Window Treatments

Conrad Window Coverings
conradshades.com
handwoven window coverings

Earthshade
earthshade.com
natural window coverings

Hartmann & Forbes
hfshades.com
bamboo, grass, jute window
coverings

Pottery and Ceramics

Health Ceramic
healthceramics.com
ceramic tableware handcrafted in
California

Jugtown Pottery
Seagrove, North Carolina
jugtownware.com
handmade salt-glaze pottery and
vases, bowls and jars in glazes made
with wood ash and local clays

Robert Compton Pottery
Bristol, Vermont
robertcomptonpottery.com
wood-fired pottery

Furniture

Berkeley Mills
Berkeley, California
berkeleymills.com
handcrafted Asian, Arts and Crafts
style furnishings

Black Canyon Restorations
blackcanyonrestorations.com
furniture made from salvaged
materials

Ekla Home
eklahome.com
sustainably made heirloom furniture

European Furniture Importers
Chicago, Illinois
eurofurniture.com
Danish furniture

Danko/Persing Enterprises
Red Lion, Pennsylvania
peterdanko.com
tables and chairs made from ply-bent
wood (in Eames tradition)

Environment Furniture
environmentfurniture.com
furniture made from reclaimed wood
and recycled and repurposed textiles

Eric Manigian
ericmanigian.com
handcrafted, salvaged-wood
furniture

Facundo Poj Design
facundopoj.com
handcrafted furniture from recycled
materials

Gary Weeks
Wimberley, Texas
garyweeks.com
handcrafted wood furniture

A Handmade Home
Los Angeles, California
ahandmadehome.com
furniture and cabinetry made from
precast sculptural concrete, reclaimed
lumber and recycled building
materials

Heritage Salvage
heritagesalvage.com
reclaimed wood furniture and green
building supplies

Home and Planet
homeandplanet.com
recycled furnishings

Natural Tree Furniture
Wilson, Kansas
smithindustries.com
handcrafted wood furniture

Robert Brandegee Designs
Pittsburgh, Pennsylvania
robertbrandegeedesigns.com
furniture made with wood from old
log structures

Rough Edges Design
Jasper, Indiana
roughedgesdesign.com
concrete table lamps, boxes and
sculptures

Rustic Furniture of Moab
Moab Utah
rusticfurnitureofmoab.com
furniture made with wood from old
barns, houses, fences and sheds

Samuel Moyer Furniture
samuelmoyerfurniture.com
reclaimed materials

Sleepywood Rustic Furniture
Berkeley Springs, West Virginia
sleepywood.com
handcrafted wood furniture

Stranger Furniture
strangerfurniture.com
salvaged wood furniture

Warisan
warisan.com
recycled teak Indonesian furniture

Whit McLeod
Arcata, California
whitmcleod.com
Arts and Crafts furniture built using
reclaimed and salvaged wood

Textiles and Upholstery

Aurora Silk
aurorasilk.com
natural fibers and dyes, cruelty-free silk

Denyse Schmidt Quilts
Bridgeport, Connecticut
dsquilts.com
quilts, fabrics, patterns, paper goods

Habitus
habitusnyc.com
cork fabric

Habu Textiles
habutextiles.com
handwoven textiles

Harmony Art
harmonyart.com
organic textiles

LIVE Textiles
livetextiles.com
organic hemp, cotton, linen, bamboo

LoooLo Textiles
looolo.ca
organic blankets and cushions

Loop
looporganic.com
organic cotton

Lulan Artisans
lulan.com
Fair Trade silks, organic cotton

Michael Miller Fabrics
michaelmillerfabrics.com
recycled fabrics, quilts, wall hangings

O Ecotextiles
oecotextiles.com
organic cotton, hemp, linen

Rawganique
rawganique.com
hemp and organic cotton

Textillery Weavers
textillery.com
handwoven throws

Twill Textiles
twilltextiles.com
organic, sustainable wool and ramie

Instyle
instyle.com.au/sustainable.html
organic wool upholstery

Candles

Aloha Bay
alohabay.com
natural palm oil/wax candles

Candle Bee Farm
candlebeefarm.com
beeswax candles

Dirt Candles
dirtcandles.com
soy candles

EcoChoices
ecochoices.com
beeswax candles, organic linens

Er'go Soy Candles
ergocandle.com
soy candles

Essence of Ahurani
alibaba.com
soy candles

GoodLight
naturalcandles.com
palm wax candles

GreenTree Home
greentreehome.com
beeswax candles

Himalayan Trading Post
himalayantradingpost.com
hand-poured soy candles

Naked Candle
nkdpure.com
soy candles

Pacifica
pacificaperfume.com
soy candles

Scandle
abodycandle.com
soy candles

Solay Wellness
natural-salt-lamps.com
natural salt lamps, soy candles

Soy Basics
soybasics.com
soy candles

Sun Beam Candles
sunbeamcandles.com
beeswax candles

Index

About the Author

Called "one of the best-informed advocates of natural living in America" by the Conservation Research Institute, ROBYN GRIGGS LAWRENCE is a passionate expert on green building and lifestyles. Lawrence, editor-at-large for *Natural Home, Mother Earth News* and *Herb Companion* magazines, has been featured in *USA Today*, the *New York Times*, *Time* magazine, the *Chicago Tribune* and on CNN. She helped launch and was the editor-in-chief of *Natural Home* from 1999 until 2010; she was previously the editor of *Mountain Living* and *Herb Companion* magazines. Lawrence lives in Boulder, Colorado, with her partner and two children.

You can read her blog at **www.motherearthnews.com/robyn**

If you have enjoyed *Simply Imperfect*, you might also enjoy other

BOOKS TO BUILD A NEW SOCIETY

Our books provide positive solutions for people who want to make a difference. We specialize in:

**Sustainable Living • Green Building • Peak Oil
Renewable Energy • Environment & Economy
Natural Building & Appropriate Technology
Progressive Leadership • Resistance and Community
Educational & Parenting Resources**

New Society Publishers

ENVIRONMENTAL BENEFITS STATEMENT

New Society Publishers has chosen to produce this book on recycled paper made with **100% post consumer waste,** processed chlorine free, and old growth free.

For every 5,000 books printed, New Society saves the following resources:[1]

14	Trees
1,304	Pounds of Solid Waste
1,435	Gallons of Water
1,872	Kilowatt Hours of Electricity
2,371	Pounds of Greenhouse Gases
10	Pounds of HAPs, VOCs, and AOX Combined
4	Cubic Yards of Landfill Space

[1]Environmental benefits are calculated based on research done by the Environmental Defense Fund and other members of the Paper Task Force who study the environmental impacts of the paper industry.

For a full list of NSP's titles, please call 1-800-567-6772 *or check out our website* at:

www.newsociety.com

NEW SOCIETY PUBLISHERS